MW00578967

Caution: Open this book only if you have tissues nearby. The stories will bring tears of sorrow for the state of our society; but thankfully, those will be washed away by tears of joy for the results of redemption and recovery. Praise God for Faith Farm and the wonderful work the staff is doing every day! Dean Webb and his team are known far and wide as innovative leaders in ministry to addicted and abused people, offering radical hospitality to the otherwise rejected and hope to the spiritually despondent. Keep those U-turns coming, my friends.

John Ashmen, President, AGRM
Association of Gospel Rescue Missions

My heart was touched as I read the powerful stories of deliverance in this book. It shows how, with God's help, faithful servants can see the evidence of changed lives. I am thankful for my friend, Dean Webb, and the team at Faith Farm Ministries who are the instruments for change!

Dan Busby, President, ECFA
Evangelical Council for Financial Accountability

After visiting Faith Farm, with its leadership, as well as with many of the graduates, I can confidently say that this is a model that should be replicated throughout the United States. Thank you to the staff, Board and contributors for the heart that you have for God and His redeeming power and for your commitment to seeing this work completed. Dean, thank you for writing this book and allowing so many powerful testimonies to be shared with so many who may never get to visit Faith Farm. This book and these testimonies should be read, seen and experienced by Believers around the world.

Ford Taylor, Founder
Transformational Leadership/FSH Group

I believe that significant and lifelong change is almost impossible on our own. I know that significant eternal life change, as described in these stories, is possible when we open our heart and allow God to change us. God also did that for me.

H. Wayne Huizenga, Jr., President
Huizenga Holdings, Inc.

In a world where drama, despair, and death abound - seeing lives dramatically changed brings real hope. It provides a clear demonstration of God's power at work in the lives of men and women who choose to follow Jesus Christ as Savior and Lord. Faith Farm serves as a bridge over troubled water; a lighthouse of hope revealing God's transforming love and grace to a watching world.

Gregg Capin, Partner
Capin Crouse LLC

We all applaud the miracles performed at Faith Farm Ministries. Their mission has been successful in turning their students' desperation into dedication and despair into deliverance. This heartfelt book shares a personal appreciation of how lives have changed.

Anita Finley, President/Publisher
BoomerTimes Magazine and Talk Show Host

When reading the testimonies of the brave souls who have dared to make a U-TURN To God through Faith Farm Ministries; I was unable to put them down. The road to recovery is fraught with difficulty and challenges. Yet these inspirational stories of how a Holy God reached down and brought hope and fulfillment touched me in the deepest recesses of my heart. It is exciting to see God is still able to change lives for His eternal purpose.

George H "Skip" Canevit, Jr. 康思奇
Christian Marine Entrepreneur Philanthropist

After reading the stories of the dramatic changes in the lives of the men and women who have graduated from Faith Farm, it caused me to focus on the importance of helping others and off the selfishness of getting my needs met. It is more blessed to give than it is to receive. Reading those stories has given me an even greater and deeper appreciation for the work Faith Farm is doing for the Kingdom of God.

Dr. Joseph Guadagnino, President
South Florida Bible College & Theological Seminary

I applaud the courage of the people who shared these powerful stories so that others suffering from addiction may hope that it is possible to turn their lives around. We can each relate these stories to our own lives. It takes amazing strength, faith and will power to change direction, but the brave individuals in this book show that it can be done. The dedication of the good people at Faith Farm Ministries to help others redirect their lives is awe-inspiring.

Rob Andy, CEO
Audia Group

Being very familiar with Faith Farm Ministries and their commitment to service in God's name, I am delighted to recommend U-TURN To God as a resource book of GREAT value. My engineering career with Proctor & Gamble and IBM; A law career practicing in the US Supreme Court; and a Banking and Finance career establishing 5 Community Banks in Florida and acting as President of Triple J. Ranch and Investment Advisors, Inc., could NOT have happened without God's help through His committed servants here on Earth. I commend Faith Farm Ministries on their God inspired work and outreach. U-TURN To God is evidence of many acts of service.

Hjalma E. Johnson

U-TURN
TO GOD

BY DEAN O. WEBB

Majesty Books

Boynton Beach, Florida

Cover Design by Judy Walters
Copyediting by Judy Walters, Cindy Webb, Amy Keefe, Joni Jones and Wayne Richardson

Majesty Books has made every effort to trace the ownership of any scripture, poems and quotes. In the event of any questions arising from the use of same, we regret any error and will be pleased to make the necessary corrections in future editions of this book.

Copyright © 2014 by Dean O. Webb
Published 2014 by Majesty Books
Boynton Beach, FL
www.MajestyBooks.com

ISBN # 978-0-9914805-2-4 (pbk)
ISBN # 978-0-9914805-1-7 (eBook)

For more information, write: Faith Farm Ministries
9538 US Highway 441, Boynton Beach, FL 33472

Table of Contents

Dedication

I dedicate this book to the thousands of men and women who have graduated from Faith Farm Ministries over the course of the last 63 years. Their lives have been transformed and regenerated through their personal commitments and the loving, redemptive power of God.

Although only a few of their stories appear in this book, each of these brave men and women graduates deserves our honor and respect. They have gone back into the world to live sober, productive, inspiring lives. Among them are fathers, mothers, sons, daughters, pastors, missionaries, nurses, Certified Addiction Counselors, half-way house managers, chefs, businessmen and women – all humble children of God, who are giving back to the world, doing God's work and being all God intended them to be.

This book is also dedicated to the hundreds of staff members of Faith Farm over the years who have given their non-judgmental, unconditional love and extraordinary effort to provide the catalyst and the environment for God's power to change the lives of their fellow human beings.

Dean O. Webb, Executive Director
Faith Farm Ministries

Foreword

Dean Webb has done an excellent job of bringing a book to the reader that testifies of the grace, mercy, and goodness of the Lord, as He stands waiting, with open arms, to welcome home His prodigal sons and daughters, whose lives have been shattered by addiction. This book is a celebration of all who have passed through the gates of Faith Farm Ministries and were set free by the power of Almighty God.

No one who made a choice to socially use a mood-altering substance intended to become addicted to it. Addiction is destructive for families, friends, finance, relationships, jobs, health, and really, anything that a person holds dear to their heart, including his own life, if he does not get help.

Addiction knows no economic or educational boundaries. It has taken men and women from the highest positions and brought them to the lowest estate. Some enter Faith Farm Ministries as homeless, and because of hopelessness, they drank or did drugs to medicate or cope with their problems. Others were of considerable wealth and lost everything. Some could not read, yet others had doctorate degrees and could speak multiple languages. From decorated military veterans and at least one CIA official, all have been brought to the knowledge of one thing … addiction is no respecter of persons, and if not stopped, it will bring all to an expected end. That is why we treat recovery very seriously, because it can be the difference between life and death.

An old Japanese proverb says, "First the man takes a drink, then the drink takes a drink, then the drink takes the man." The same can

11

be true for any mood-altering substance, when a man or a woman has an addictive personality.

Webster's New World Dictionary defines rehabilitation as, "to restore to rank, reputation, etc., which one has lost; to put back in good condition."

Faith Farm Ministries is NOT committed to putting "back in good condition." We are committed to regeneration. Webster's defines regeneration as, "spiritually reborn; renewed; to cause to be spiritually reborn; to be made anew."

We have found, since the beginning of this ministry, that there is only one thing that can cause a person to make a permanent "U TURN" in their life. There is only one thing that can cause a person to be spiritually reborn. There is only one thing that can change a heart. And, there is only one thing that can change a man or woman from the inside out. That one thing is a personal, passionate pursuit of the Lord Jesus Christ. We found that freedom from addiction is a by-product of that pursuit.

The program, in its simplicity, is an organized opportunity for the above to happen. In its complexity of almost 63 years of development, it has become a powerful, therapeutic community.

In the Bible, Joseph's brothers sold him into slavery and he ended up in Egypt. He found favor and became second in command, in all of Egypt, only to Pharaoh. He was able to save his father and brothers and many others from starvation during a horrible time of famine. In the end, he said to his brothers in Genesis 50:20;

> But as for you, you meant evil against me; but God meant it for good, in order to bring it about as it is this day, to save many people alive.

Interestingly, Satan has used the evil of addiction to try and destroy the lives of many; but God has used the enemy's ploy to capture some of the most gifted and talented men and women in the world, set them free by His power, and use them for His glory.

In John 10:10, Jesus said;

> *The thief does not come except to steal, and to kill, and to destroy. I have come that they might have life, and that they might have it more abundantly.*

In 1959, my father, Rev. Gurnade Brown, was asked by the Founder of Faith Farm Ministries, Rev. Garland "Pappy" Eastham, to answer the call to pastor and direct the original work, located in Ft. Lauderdale, Florida, which at that time was called The Ft. Lauderdale Rescue Mission. My father did answer the call, and our family moved from Indiana to Florida; at that time, I was 6 years old. Growing up in this ministry, and later, after college, serving on staff, I was privileged to witness with my own eyes, the miracle of changed lives through the regenerating, transforming power of our Lord Jesus Christ.

Pastor Mike Brown, President
Faith Farm Ministries Board of Directors

Preface

I will never forget the breathtaking experience of standing in the Cecil B. Day Butterfly Conservatory at Callaway Gardens, Georgia. The two-story, all glass dome was so quiet, yet filled with hundreds of butterflies flying in all directions as darting movements of color, but no sound. My conflicting senses, seeing a lot of rapid movement without hearing any sound, was a strange experience.

I began to stare at a smaller glass enclosure containing a row of caterpillars in various stages of graduating maturity, left to right. They were all attached to a suspended twig. The most mature cocoon on the right began to twitch and then shake. Eventually, the cocoon began to expose a slight crack. After much effort, the wings of a beautiful butterfly became noticeable. A little while later, a beautiful butterfly emerged from the shell with its wings beginning to move. Before long, the wings flapped more quickly, and the butterfly began to fly.

The dictionary describes metamorphosis as "a transformation, as by magic; a marked change in appearance, character, condition, or function." Well, I had just witnessed one of these miracles on earth ... the metamorphosis of an ugly caterpillar becoming a beautiful butterfly. It was amazing to witness such a transformation in real life. Likewise, I get to observe and hear testimonies of lives radically changed by God at graduations that occur every six weeks at three different Farms. I simply could not resist somehow exposing this transformation of life that occurs at Faith Farm to the world. We provide the place ... God does the work of change.

In this book, you will read testimonies of broken lives that have been changed by the power of God. Students entering the program have been abused, broken, prostituted, or convicted as criminals; some having served prison time. Others come as children from loving homes and a church background, but were sidetracked into drugs and alcohol by peer pressure. Some have been upstanding citizens who were involved in some kind of accident or sustained an injury that led to an addiction to prescription pain medicines and have lost everything. Others have been very well off financially and had their lives destroyed because of their addictions. Regardless of their circumstances, they have made a complete "U-TURN" in their lives. These are stories of lives transformed by the power of unconditional love and the grace of God. Faith Farm lives out its purpose for our students daily: *"Restoring Hope... One Life at a Time"* and these are their stories. Please enjoy reading them.

Dean O. Webb, Executive Director
Faith Farm Ministries

Acknowledgements

There are so many people involved in the writing of a book such as this. Of course, without the Faith Farm student graduates of the program providing their stories and permission to use them, this book would not be possible.

Most of the credit must go to Judy Walters, who designed the cover, and provided much needed suggestions on all facets of the book and its design. Judy acquired the Majesty Books name, set up the website domain, acquired the ISBN numbers and facilitated the publishing. Thanks, Judy.

Thanks also, to Joni Jones, a graduate of the women's program who tirelessly listened to hundreds of recorded graduation speeches and laboriously transcribed them into print for proofing. She also researched publishing and provided the framework around the publishing of this book, from publishing specs to the formatting of the pages. I also want to thank Judy Walters, Amy Keefe, and Wayne Richardson for copyediting.

And, thank you to my daughter, Catherine Webb Williams, for the creative title for the book. Also, thank you to every staff member, who provided the work structure that allowed me to work this book into my schedule.

Finally, I express a very loving thank you to my wife, Cindy, for her unconditional, selfless support by graciously allowing me to be absent from our weekends together in order for me to work on this project. This is a work of love by many people, who strongly desire that the transformation of lives that occur at Faith Farm Ministries be allowed to be told to the public.

Dean O. Webb, Executive Director
Faith Farm Ministries

Introduction

These are the actual transcripts of recorded speeches given on graduation day before a live audience. By reading these transcripts, it's like you are present in the audience. Testimonies have only been altered for punctuation, grammar, or clarification. Therefore, there will be references to Faith Farm staff members, other students and classmates in the program or family members in the audience. Also, gratitude or apologies are sometimes expressed to parents and other family members present at graduation. Most last names of students and staff have been omitted to honor anonymity and confidentiality, with few obvious exceptions.

Quoted scriptures come from a variety of different versions of the bible, as chosen by the graduates. Some have indicated which version they were quoting, and some did not. If the testimony is a letter received from a graduate instead of their graduation speech, it will be so noted. We claim poetic license for the occasional unedited slang and jargon used, because correcting it just didn't seem right! We couldn't have said it any better!

When you read about someone being "Baker-Acted", the Baker Act is a means of providing individuals with emergency services and temporary detention for mental health evaluation and treatment when required, either on a voluntary or an involuntary basis.

These speeches are testimonies to the miraculous life changes that can occur when those who have succumbed to the addictive lifestyle are sequestered voluntarily in the loving, non-judgmental environment of a Faith Farm campus. Here, they are taught about who they are in Christ and the power they can experience by accepting Him into their lives. They are taught about addictive behavior and causes of addiction. They learn that they need to forgive and to resolve anger issues. They learn that God has a purpose for their lives. They are reminded that it's not how they *start* out in life that will be remembered, but the legacy of how they *finish*.

Slowly, God lovingly changes their thoughts about themselves and about God. They experience the power of forgiveness. Also, for the first time, they come to know of the hurt and pain experienced by family members and loved ones as a result of their addiction. While Faith Farm provides the place, the students must provide their own motivation to change. Each graduate is a miracle of change through God's grace.

We hope you enjoy reading about some of the transformed lives created by God in the environment of Faith Farm.

Dean O. Webb, Executive Director
Faith Farm Ministries

Emily

Please join me in a Word of prayer: Dear Heavenly Father, thank you for gathering us all here today at this appointed time. Please be with me as I share this testimony. Allow my words to touch someone's heart today and glorify you and what you've done in my life. In Jesus' name, I pray. Amen.

I was raised in Oklahoma, and I grew up in a loving family. I was blessed as a child with memories of family vacations, traveling, and quality time spent together. We went to church every Sunday, and a seed was sown at a young age. I was baptized as an infant by my grandfather. Both my grandparents and great-grandparents were ministers and missionaries. I am truly grateful for their heritage and their legacy.

When I was 10 years old, my parents divorced. I had a poor self-image and low self-esteem, and I was rebellious. I started drinking at the age of 14. Soon, I was smoking marijuana, partying, sneaking out of the house and lying to my parents. I knew right from wrong, but the thrill of doing something I should *not* be doing was a driving force behind my reckless behavior.

I made straight A's and graduated at the top of my class. I excelled in many sports, especially soccer. Once, I was even named the number one goal keeper in the State of Oklahoma in Class 4A. I was an American girl with the American dream: Go to college; have a successful career; marry a rich doctor and have a big family, a big house with a white picket fence and live happily ever after. But there was something missing inside of me. Not knowing what it was, I filled that void with drugs and alcohol and everything else to satisfy the emptiness. At the age of 17, I was raped, and I never told anyone. The shame and guilt I carried from that only sent me further into my addiction and depression.

I was accepted to the University of Oklahoma in the fall of 2005, and I thought I could start over. I was wrong. I was not ready, and I went looking for the parties instead of focusing on school. College gave me the opportunity to try as many different types of drugs as there were available. In my first semester, I was sanctioned for alcohol and kicked out of the dorms for smoking pot.

A year later, I moved back to my hometown to play soccer for a university, thinking that the structure and my soccer coaches would help me get my act together. Again, that failed to be true. I continued to struggle in college and sought help through psychiatry. I was prescribed medication to cope with real life problems, only to set me up for more failure. I did well for a while and actually got my grades up. I was ready to enter nursing school when real life happened, and I fell apart.

I found comfort in the numbing effects of methamphetamine. Within in a year, I was on the streets, selling to live and living to stay high. I alienated myself away from my family and friends, and I surrounded myself with drugs, money and guns. I had become an IV user and a drug dealer. To top it off, I was lured into my Prince Charming's arms, under the protective covering of a con artist. I was soon exposed to rage, jealousy, and control I had never known before ... threats to harm me and those I loved, if I were to leave him. Soon, I was isolated from everyone and kept under constant watch. I was broken down into a person I didn't even know. John 10:10 states:

> The thief does not come except to steal, kill and to destroy.

I lost control of myself, and I was being controlled by someone else. I knew I needed more protection. So, I obtained a Glock 9mm, a box of shells and a handful of full-metal jackets.

With the sound of the loud crack of the front door breaking in by the sheriff's department, my thoughts were, "This is all over." On my way to jail, I ingested a lethal amount of meth and cocaine. Shortly after they placed me in the cell, I overdosed. I was rushed to the emergency room. I don't remember much, but the doctors and police were stunned when there were no signs of drugs in my stomach. I look back now, and I realize I was not *arrested* that day. I was *rescued!*

But, jail time and rehab were still not enough to stop me from going back to my old ways. I knew I needed more, and I knew in my heart that God had spared my life numerous times. I began to seek Him.

Jeremiah 29:11-14 says:

> *For I know the thoughts that I think toward you, says the Lord, thoughts of peace and not of evil, to give you a future and a hope. Then you will call upon Me and go and pray to Me, and I will listen to you. And you will seek Me and find Me, when you search for Me with all your heart. I will be found by you, says the Lord, and I will bring you back from your captivity; I will gather you from all the nations and from all the places where I have driven you, says the Lord, and I will bring you to the place from which I cause you to be carried away captive.*

The plans the enemy had to destroy me, God is now using to glorify Himself. It is by the gift of His grace, forgiveness, love and unending mercy that I am able to stand here in front of all of you today and say that I am a grateful child of God and a daughter of the true King. Though I used to be a slave to sin, I am honored and privileged to be a slave to righteousness for His name's sake. You see, Romans 5:8 says,

> But God demonstrates His own love toward us in that
> while we were still sinners, Christ died for us.

I thank God for Faith Farm every day. The decision to come here was the best decision I have made. It was life or death, and Jesus calls on us to choose life. Faith Farm helped me restore my mind, body and soul. I rededicated my life to Jesus as my Lord and Savior. I was baptized here (at Faith Farm). Although at first, I didn't understand why everyone was raising their hands and praising God, I learned that it's all worship … and it feels good to worship God. I am happier than I have been my whole life. I have that real true peace inside my heart that only comes from God. I know that I have a Heavenly Father who is always watching over me. For the new students, I encourage you stay. It takes time to change, especially to change the way we think. Proverbs 3:5-6 says,

> Trust in the Lord with all your heart, and lean not on
> your own understanding; in all your ways acknowledge
> Him, and He shall direct your paths.

I have decided to stay as an extended student for 6 more months. This gives me the opportunity to grow and develop character and to give back to the place that gave me everything.

Author's Note: After her graduation, Emily distinguished herself as an Intern to the COO/Development Director. Emily trained to write grants for submission, while going to college at night. She often gives her testimony to visitors, and has even delivered the sermon in a Wednesday night service at the Boynton Beach campus church. Emily is a totally changed person. In 2014, Emily married a Faith Farm alumni, who is serving in the US Army on active duty.

Stewart

The destruction all started when I was 10. My best friend was killed in a DUI auto accident. I never could get over it. At age 12, I started drinking; age 13 smoking pot; age 14 was cocaine; age 15 dealing drugs and leaving home, never to return. Living on the edge, I had become a very violent person, hurting anyone who got in my way.

At age 17, I got a girl pregnant. She had my son, Cory. Now I was 18. God knew I wasn't fit to be a father, and Cory died at 6 months old of SIDS (sudden infant death syndrome). The sick part about this is I was so entrenched in my addiction; I was relieved, even happy I didn't have to buy diapers or formula. Now, I thought, I had reason to act like a maniac. Sad, but I didn't have the courage to speak this until today.

Shortly in the aftermath, I met my ex-wife, who despised cocaine. But, as usual, I lied through several years of marriage. Coming from upstate New York and moving to Florida in 1993, I thought the move would change my life, not realizing I needed to change the inside of me before I could make the new outside work. I thought I was doing the right thing; working, not using cocaine, but still drinking and smoking pot. I went 7 years without using cocaine. Then it happened! I had a full-blown relapse.

During surgery for a broken back, I received 6 screws, 2 rods, and a titanium cage in my back. I was mad at the world and God. Why me? My mom told me that God has His reasons for all things to happen. Well, I was pretty mad at God. Four months after surgery; in 2004, my ex-wife caught me using cocaine. It was over. I left home only to get on the super-highway to hell.

I met a new girlfriend, Nikki. We were a perfect recipe for disaster. Now smoking about $500 - $1,000 a day worth of cocaine, we partied for ten months together. Nikki had two children, ages 14 and 16. On January 5, 2005, in a drug deal gone south, I had an altercation with Nikki's brother. He tried to shoot me, and then proceeded to run me over with his truck. What a night! Despite the cops, breaking a screw in my back, and the whole nine yards, I refused medical treatment. I couldn't go to the hospital—I had dope at home to smoke!

On January 13, 2005, Nikki took me to the hospital and dropped me off. I got out the next morning, and she was nowhere to be found. I called a cab only to go to my home and find her dead hanging in the closet. She couldn't take the lifestyle any more. She left me a note and a voicemail about how I sold her soul to the devil! I cried out to God, and He heard me.

Despite all of this, I continued to get high until I ran out of money and picked up eight felonies and three misdemeanors. Off to jail I went, praise God! I spent ten months there still fighting the urge to use. God introduced me to some good people who told me, "Only God can set you free from the life that you are living." It was suggested to me to go to Faith Farm Ministries. "That is where you will find what you need," said Pastor Al and Counselor Nolli. I defeated the odds with the charges brought against me. I realized that I could have done 47 years in prison. It could only be God at work - no money, no one to help me, except God.

As I pled to the judge, he gave me 5 years of probation and suspended my payment of over $30,000 worth of restitution and fines, and $10,000 in child support I owed. The judge offered me a ride to Faith Farm Ministries. I took him up on it.

On November 17, 2005, over the loudspeaker in St. Lucie County jail, the corrections officer said, "Number 351, pack your stuff, it's time to go." I was so excited to start my new life. As I was dropped off, handcuffed and shackled at the front door of Faith Farm, men came to me and said, "You are in good hands now." Little did I know what a work God was doing!

Life was great and exciting for about a month. Then I began to become somewhat ungrateful. The staff would ask me to do stuff that I thought was totally ridiculous. Like trim weeds with scissors. I know I packed my bags at least three times thinking I had some kind of answer; where I was going, I still don't know. I had no home, and I thought my family hated me.

With no phone privileges, I had no way to try to make things right at home, but that is the way God set it up. I had to learn to depend on Him! Christmas came. We were allowed five minutes to call home. Yes, finally I can get right with my family. But when I called, my ex-wife told me what a no-good "blah, blah, blah" I was, and that she hoped that I rotted in hell. Wow! What a blow that was! I was angry with myself, God, and everyone around me.

After about a month of not being very nice to my fellow students, the pastor—my hero—sat me down. He let me know what time it was and asked if I wanted to continue with my program. He told me to stop trying to fix my life; God has already fixed it through the gift of His son, Jesus, and when I am ready to receive the grace He died for, my life would begin to change.

Two months later, a staff member approached me on a Monday morning going into Class 4, (approximately 6 months into the program), and said, "I have a message for you. Your ex-wife called and said she was coming on Wednesday to pick you up to see your children!" I dropped to my knees in the hallway and cried

29

uncontrollably for at least thirty minutes. God was delivering on the promise Pastor told me about. Now the miracle thing was on.

That Wednesday morning, my ex didn't show up as I waited out front for her. It was 9:15 AM. Then I saw the black Hummer coming down the road. It was my ex-father-in-law. Now let me tell you, I hurt this man bad. When God is at work, you better hang on. This was the last thing I would expect. Crying, he got out with tears and said, "Son, it's time to come home and see your children." Well, the rest of my days at Faith Farm were great. God was doing a work every day in my life and continues to this very day.

Alyssa

I arrived at Faith Farm on May 8, 2010. I am 27 years old, and my addiction began 13 years ago, when I was 14 years old. I have tried to be rid of this addiction for years. I have been in and out of treatment centers, detox facilities, AA and outpatient counseling, and I have been to jail twice. I even tried moving from place to place, but nothing ever worked. I could never understand why I always ran back to the bottle and the drugs. For years, I thought that something was wrong with me and that I could never change. I had completely lost all hope. I have suffered many consequences because of my addiction. I am going to share some of my past with you today to show what God has saved me from, and how He has set me free.

I have been an alcoholic since the first time I ever took a drink. Black-out drinking became normal to me. In fact, I would black-out almost every time I drank. But somehow, drinking was not enough. By the time I was 18, I ended up in a treatment center for a cocaine addiction. I spent 28 days there. The first week I was out, I was high.

Two years later, I moved to Florida, where I was introduced to pharmaceuticals. I figured they were legal and I had never been addicted to them before so why not? Little did I know what kind of damage they would do to my life! This was when everything took a huge turn for the worse. I began mixing pills with alcohol on a daily basis. On July 4, 2005, I had taken some pills and then gone out to a bar with my co-workers. As usual, I was in a black-out.

The next thing I knew, I was lying on the side of the road covered in blood and my car was smashed into a tree. I have absolutely no recollection of the accident or how I got out of the car. The passenger, who was a very close friend of mine, was not wearing a seatbelt and was ejected from the car on impact, landing in the street unconscious. He was airlifted to a trauma center, and I was told that he had a 40% chance of surviving. By the grace of God, this man is alive today with no permanent damage. If he had died, I would've had to live with the guilt of killing my friend, and I would have faced a minimum 15 year prison sentence at 20 years old. I would not be standing here a free and saved woman today. I know God's angels saved us that night. But, unfortunately, almost killing myself and someone else was not enough to stop my addiction.

By the age of 24, I ended up back in treatment again. I thought I wanted to get clean, but I was wrong. I did not completely surrender to the program, and I wanted to do it "my way." I ended up meeting a guy who was also in the program. Secretly, we became a couple. We were there together for 3 months until one day he ended up getting kicked out for using. Foolishly, I followed him and left, too. That night we were drunk.

Three days later we bought some drugs, and I took so much that I don't remember anything from that night. Sadly, we thought we could handle it. After we had gone to sleep, I woke up in the middle of the night to get a drink. I came back into the room only to find that his whole body was stiff. I turned on the lights, and I saw that he was dead. I was told that his heart had stopped some time during the night due to a drug overdose from mixing pills. I don't know how long I laid there while he was dead. Selfishly, I was angry that God took him and not me. We had taken the same amount of drugs, and I didn't understand why I was still alive. I felt like I was left on this earth as a punishment to live with the guilt of this man's death, and I felt completely responsible. I blamed myself for his death because I supplied the drugs.

This guilt only fueled my addiction even more. I became so damaged by these painful memories, that using drugs to the extreme was the only way I could get through every day and night. I thought drugs were the only way to numb the pain. When I didn't think a bottom could get any worse, it did. I began to use drugs intravenously. By February 2010, I ended up back in detox with no job, homeless, and my family wanted nothing to do with me. I was utterly alone. All I had was a backpack knocking at the door of detox. I knew that I needed something different than what I had tried before to get me clean. I desperately needed a Mighty Savior.

I came to Faith Farm broken, afraid and confused. I couldn't accept love from anyone, and I didn't understand why all these women were hugging me telling me they loved me the first day I got here. To me, it seemed like they were all on drugs! But it was not drugs that made them happy. It was God's love flowing through them and pouring onto me. He knew I needed it. I did not have a relationship with God when I came here, so praying and asking for help was hard at first. But after surrendering and earnestly seeking Him, it's like talking to a friend. His Word really came alive to me when I read Isaiah 26:3-4,

> You will keep him in perfect peace, whose mind is stayed on you, because he trusts you. Trust in the Lord forever, for in Yahweh, the Lord, is everlasting strength.

Peace is what I have been searching for all these years. And, through prayer and His Word, He has truly brought peace to my heart. I no longer re-live the painful memories of my past. God has set me free! Galatians 5:1 says,

> Christ has set us free. He wants us to enjoy freedom. So stand firm. Don't let the chains of slavery hold you again.

Thanks to God and Faith Farm, I can stand before you and say that I no longer have to believe the lies I have let Satan tell me for years. I am not lost and confused. I do have a purpose and that is to worship the Lord. I don't have to feel guilty because I am already forgiven. I am not unwanted and unworthy of love because God, Himself, told me that He loves me. Deuteronomy 7:8 states,

> But because the Lord loves you, and because He would keep the oath, which He swore to your fathers, the Lord has brought you out with a mighty hand, and redeemed you from the house of bondage. (NKJV)

He has truly redeemed my life. He has brought me from being homeless with a needle in my arm to proclaiming my love for Him in a church by being baptized in His Name. Only God, Himself, can bring us out of our pits of despair. We have tried everything else. Now, He has brought us to Him, not as a last resort, but as a first chance at life. You know how we all have felt like we've never belonged? I believe that God didn't want us to feel like we belonged anywhere else, because He wants us to know that we belong to Him.

Author's Note: *Below is an update received from Alyssa, March 2014:*

God has continued to bless my life in so many ways since I have moved on from Faith Farm. My family has been restored. I now have the relationships with them that I have always wanted. God even increased my family, as I was married in August 2011, to my awesome husband, Eric. Together, we have started our own business and are flourishing successfully. God honors tithing. We have planted ourselves at a church that has a program for addiction. We have been called into the ministry and have been working there as mentors to the men and women in the program. God has gifted me with a powerful testimony, and He is utilizing it to help others.

Thanks to Faith Farm, I am equipped with the tools necessary to carry out this ministry. Thank you, God and Faith Farm, for saving and changing my life into more than I ever thought it could be.

Daniel

Revelation 12:11:

They overcame him by the Blood of the Lamb and the words of their testimony.

Father God, thank you for delivering me from the darkness I was in. Father, let all the praise be unto You today, Father, and everything You've done in my life, Father. Let me turn to You when I need You, as You will always be there for me. May the words of my mouth glorify You. In Jesus' name, Amen.

How does this living, walking, breathing, testimony put together thirty-one years of life's experiences in this ten-month experience that has truly transformed me and changed me and my life into a five minute speech? Only through the power of the Holy Spirit! This morning, I will share with you, who I was in my addiction, the consequences of my addiction, and how I found Jesus Christ; or, better yet, how He found me, and who I am today in Jesus Christ. To know who I am today, you must first come to know where I am from.

I am from Miami originally, born and raised. I am a product of an Argentine father and a Spanish Italian mother from Brooklyn...forget about it *(laugh)*! I was raised in a family with two brothers, known as the twin towers, and one sister. I know that I came from a family that loves me very much. My parents got divorced at a very young age, and I know that this had a profound effect on my emotional state.

Growing up, I was an athlete. I realize now that I used sports as a means to not deal with the issues or emotions that were affecting me. I also realize that I was very obsessive compulsive in my behavior. The positive is that this allowed me to get a college education and play college ball, but it was also the fuel to my addiction. It says in I Peter 5:8;

> *Be sober; be vigilant; because your adversary the devil walks about like a roaring lion, seeking whom he may devour.* (NIV)

Let me tell you about my addiction. My addiction began in its roots as I was introduced to music; as I was introduced to the electronic music scene. In the music scene, I found myself abusing drugs such as ecstasy, LSD, GHB, and cocaine. These drugs, combined with my obsessive-compulsive behavior and my addiction to hard liquor, soon became a destructive combination. I would soon find myself consumed by the Miami Beach nightclub scene and the underground music festivals.

This hardcore drug scene left me with a massive addiction to cocaine and alcohol. I was on a deep, dark path to self-destruction. This glamorous social lifestyle soon drove me to a place of solitude, isolation, and depression. I would suffer the consequences of losing functionality and losing six great jobs in the past ten years.

My addiction was severe. I became the addict with binges that almost caused me to go blind in my left eye. I became the addict who completely passed out behind the wheel of a driving car, barely escaping death. I became the addict who took a butcher knife six inches from my heart playing with suicide. I became the addict who could no longer fight this battle, one night taking all the pills in my house just to not wake up.

I lied, I cheated, I stole and I hurt many people, especially those who cared most for me—my family. At this time, I would like to recognize my family who are in the back pews. I would just like to apologize to you guys one last time and tell you that I'm deeply sorry that I hurt you. You truly did not deserve to go through what I put you through. I'm sorry.

Revelation 3:20 states,

> *Behold, I stand at the door and knock. If anyone hears my voice and opens the door, I will come in and dine with him, and he with Me.* (NIV)

Now I will tell you what Faith Farm did for me and how I found God here. Faith Farm is truly a work of God, and I am eternally grateful for having come to this place. This place taught me so much about myself, about the flaws that I had in me and it taught me to humble myself.

I Peter 5:6 states,

> *Therefore, humble yourself into the mighty hand of God, that He may exalt you in due time casting all your cares upon Him for He cares for you.* (NIV)

I remember! I remember those calls I made to the intake office for three weeks trying to get in here. I remember after being on a two-day binge, being told, "Do you have any Christian music around?" I didn't know what that meant at the time, and I didn't think the intake counselor was serious. Now, I know that we're called to worship God. That's the purpose of our lives. Our lives are to worship the Man, the Being and the Existence that sent me here.

This place taught me to grow in my humility. This is for the guys, and I'm speaking to every single one of you: I love every single one of you guys, and I look at all of you and you know what I see? I see true men of God. You might not see it yet, but this program will start to tear down those walls...tear down those walls of your heart so you can receive Jesus Christ inside of you. That's what matters. This isn't about work. This isn't about money. This is about your lives. I see some of the brightest, most intelligent, most articulate men I've ever seen in my life sitting here. The devil just got the best of us.

Now, it's our job. Every single one of you guys, it's your job to receive and to give away what you have received. How do you do this? You do this by honoring God. Faith Farm taught me how to honor God. They always say, "I've heard it before I came here," and "There's no instructions on how to live life." There *are* instructions on how to live life. There *is* a way to be a man.

> *When I was a child, I spoke as a child. I thought as a child. When I became a man I put away childish things.*
> *(NIV)*

This is the Book of Life. *(Daniel raises the Bible in his hand.)* In this Book I found myself. Through this process, I received the power of the Holy Spirit; the most amazing power that any human being can live with. It's so overpowering that one day my body could not even consume it. I'm so grateful I live with this power today.

See, the same Spirit that lives in Jesus Christ lives in every single person sitting here today. We can all live in victory through this power. So I say to all men in this congregation, I love all of you, I truly do. What have you done for Christ today? What are you doing to remain sober? What are you doing to remain functional? You can only do this through the power of Jesus Christ.

Now, I have people here that I wanted to thank, because the staff has been so great to me and I think there are so many awesome, awesome men of God here. Everyone serves their purpose. The only person that I'm going to personally thank and I would like to honor is my Pastor. His love for God has been an example for me of how to love God. And Pastor, I truly love you and you're truly, truly a man of

God. And you're humble subtleness … such an example of the ways of Jesus Christ. So I would like to honor you today.

The Pastor gave a sermon on changing your destiny. Well, today my destiny has truly been changed. I choose today not to go home. I choose to stay at Faith Farm. I choose to stay here because I know I have been called to ministry. I know I've been called to give my life to Jesus Christ and touch as many people as I can. When I stand before Jesus Christ, and I can only imagine; I want Him to look me in the eyes and say,"I'm proud of you, my son. "

Author's Note: *Daniel now runs the Boca House, a halfway house in Boca Raton, Florida, for men out of recovery. Daniel was one of our guest speakers at our annual Homecoming celebration on February 9, 2014. On March 5th, I brought Daniel to be a guest with me on the Boomer Times Radio Show to tell his story. Daniel's desire is to be in ministry.*

Phyllis

I would like to begin with two scriptures that have carried me through this season of my life. The first is Jeremiah 29:11:

> *For I know the plans I have for you, says The Lord; plans to prosper you and not harm you; plans to give you a future and a hope.*

The second scripture is Isaiah 40:31:

> *But those who trust in The Lord will renew their strength; they shall mount up with wings like eagles, they shall run and not be weary, they shall walk and not faint.* (NKJV)

When I first came to Faith Farm, I believed that I had fallen so far from grace that God would not forgive me this time. I have since learned that is a lie. I also carried a lot of guilt and shame upon arriving at Faith Farm. I am a mother who was raised by a strong and beautiful Christian woman. I should have known better. I should have made better choices. My first bad choice was made at 16 years old when I started smoking weed. Cocaine came shortly after, and I thought, "I'll never be free of this." Anger and self-hatred followed and continued to grow. I found out I was pregnant with my daughter when I was 25 years old. It was only by the grace of God that I was able to leave cocaine alone.

I attended church with my mom, and things seemed to be going well for a while. Then I made the fatal mistake of thinking I could do this all on my own. That was the biggest mistake I have ever made in my life.

Trying to fill a tremendous void in my life, I smoked more weed. When that didn't work, I tried to numb the pain with xanax. Still feeling the pain, I moved up to pain pills and thought, "I'll never be free of this." All the while, the anger and the self-hatred still grew inside of me.

About 5 years ago, I discovered oxycotin. I maintained what I thought was an okay amount for a while; still thinking, "I'll never be free of this." About 2 ½ years ago, my brother committed suicide, and that is when my life really took a turn for the worse. By this time, I was up to almost 20 pills per day, and I knew I would never be free of this ... or so I thought at the time!

I committed a crime, felony larceny, and when the police came to my house, I was arrested in front of my daughter. I went to jail and was there over a month. Within five months, I had violated probation twice. Still, that was not enough to get or keep me clean. At this point, I was convinced that I would never be free from drugs, hate, anger and rage. Every time I thought of the look on my daughter's face as I was taken away by the police, the self-hatred grew.

I came to Faith Farm thinking I would learn how to not get high when things got rough. But, praise be to God, I have learned so much more. I have learned who I am in Christ. I've learned to hold my head up high, be a Godly woman, a better mother, respect authority and honor my mother. By the grace of God, my mother and my children will never have to suffer at my hands again.

So, giving all glory and honor to God, I can finally say, "Free at last! Free at last! Thank God almighty! I'm free at last!"

Michael

Author's Note: *Michael had been through 34 different treatment centers trying to get off drugs before he finally came to Faith Farm. However, Faith Farm was his first faith-based recovery program. After 6 months here, Michael dropped dead on the steps of the church, and was taken to the hospital emergency room ICU. He was there for 2 weeks before being brought back to consciousness. Then he had a heart pacemaker operation. Michael has said he wants to spend the rest of his life at Faith Farm to give back to helping other men and saving their lives, the way his was saved. Michael runs the extended program for basic program graduates, Omega Work and Omega School, obtaining jobs for them and scholarships to attend college or trade schools.*

My name is Michael. I was born February 10, 1951, in Manhattan Beach, Brooklyn, New York. I remember living close to the ocean, and how the sea salt smell filled the air. Growing up in this part of the city was peaceful and calm. We had one public school and every young student walked to school every day. Life was fun and simple. On Sundays, we made family trips to Manhattan to Radio City Music Hall, the movie theaters, and different restaurants. New York City was the most exciting place to visit, and then we went back to the quiet of the beach. I was a happy kid and had lots of friends. My father was a dentist, and mom was a housewife. Dad went off to work every day. Mom took care of me and my sister Patti, who was 3 years younger than me.

In the summer of my fifth grade year, my mom and dad called us into the living room for a family talk. We were moving to a new part of Brooklyn. I felt my little heart drop to my feet. I was just a young boy that had his first real heart pain. So, we moved away from Manhattan Beach to a new, strange neighborhood, the Midwood section of Brooklyn, the block of East 21st between Ave J and Ave I. I was to start in a new school in the sixth grade. I went from a happy kid to a not so happy kid. For some reason, I was put in a class with "hooligan" students, not wanting to learn the lessons. So I became a junior "yahoo," not fitting my personality. I did it to just fit in. I started to make new friends, found my way in the new neighborhood. Mom and dad started to fight more and more. I started junior high school and started to like the girls. I was 12 years old not knowing what my future was. My home life was scaring me because of the fighting between my folks. I was not doing well in school and getting into trouble. Life was hard for this 13 year old. When I was still in junior high school, music was becoming the big thing ... The Beatles and The Rolling Stones. I made it to high school, made new friends, forgot about Manhattan Beach, and mom and dad were still fighting.

In 1967, drugs surfaced in my life. I started with pills, pot and pharmaceutical drugs—pot from South America and Thailand, and hash from Nepal and Afghanistan. It was wild and free times in New York City. I was just passing in my grades. I moved to the senior class.

It was 1969, the summer of Woodstock. I grew my hair long and just wanted to be left alone to "do my thing," which was really nothing constructive at all. I was just wasting my time thinking I was having fun! Everything I did was based on getting high. The Vietnam War was raging, and I was summoned to go to the Army post to be drafted. To my amazement, I was rejected because I had high blood pressure. Now, I was happy and free of the draft, as I was coming to the end of high school in the year 1969. My life was a mess; mixed up and drugged up, but I had a great girlfriend.

I was very troubled. I was sent to a psychiatrist to find out why I was such a confused young man. Why did I just want to get stoned and not go to a good college and learn how to be a proper young man? I hated when my parents argued, and the only relief I had was to get intoxicated. The new drug in town was cocaine and quaaludes. The parties became wild. I stole, I lied and I did what I had to do to get money to buy drugs. I was an outlaw in my folks' eyes.

Finally, it was graduation time 1969, and everyone took off for college. I went to a school in Delaware, filled with men and women like me—a party school. We would drive to New York City every Friday night and return with drugs for the week to come. It was a waste of dad's money, and I learned nothing. Things were still wild and free. I lasted at this school one year and was asked to leave.

I wanted so bad to move out west. I went out west many times. I loved being on the road, meeting people. The west is a beautiful place … the mountains, the ocean, so different from the east coast. I was still getting high; learning nothing, hustling money back and forth to California.

Deep in the back of my mind was this pretty girl, Barbara. She was up in Boston going to an all-women's school. I think I loved this girl, so I went to Boston to find her. It was another world, and I was an outcast. But, she did miss me and did like me. How strange that was. Still today, I can't understand what she saw in me. Jumping ahead, she transferred to NYU in lower Manhattan. I moved in with her, and we were married in 1975. I worked in the city, and she became a social worker. I worked at a place called Fine Arts Furniture. We had fun times in the big apple and moved to Brooklyn Heights.

One day, her father took us out to dinner and said, "Son, how would you like to work for me?" He had a plumbing supply business in Fort Greene, Brooklyn: a rough, all-black, Spanish neighborhood. I said OK! I would give it a try, and I left my job in New York City. The job was not easy, and it was in a scary part of town. We were the only white people around. I was scared silly. I learned the business, and I

47

made money. We saved money and built a home up in the Catskill Mountains. One day, my father in-law passed out at work and never returned. He passed away. I was left to run the business. God does have a sense of humor. To top it off, this was one of the largest drug areas of the city.

I was the big business man making money and helping the poorer people, and they loved me because I got high...it was all so crazy. We had two children. Life was not so bad, except that I still got high on pot, pills and coke. At night, I would drink myself to sleep, because I was so wound up from cocaine. I don't know how we did it—running a business, being parents and getting stoned. One winter day, I asked one of the street fellows if he could get me a bag of heroin. He looked at me kind of funny and said, "Sure thing." I gave him $20, and he returned with 2 bags. I took the bags up to my office and sniffed one of them. A couple of hours later, I did the other one. I never felt so good. All my pain went away. I was on top of the world. I gave up cocaine, pot, pills, and just wanted heroin. It all happened so fast. I became addicted to this white power.

My world became a complete disaster. The family found out that I gave some to my wife, and she became addicted to this white powder. It was a horrible time. She broke down, went to her brother and "spilled the beans." Her mother and brother went into action, hired a lawyer and got her into treatment. I was fired. Everything was sold. The store closed, and I was sent to my first treatment center.

Kicking a heroin habit is probably the hardest task I ever did in my life. I can't tell you what that pain was like. I could not do it. I left the treatment center and moved into a car in a gas station right across the street from the closed business. I had nothing left, and I did not care anymore. I called friends, borrowed money and used heroin. I was now a "street junkie." I walked the streets begging for money. Finally, with the help of my dad, I got on SSI (Social Security Income) free government money. The country house was sold. I was given a small amount of money and the rest went to the ex-wife and children. I used all my money on drugs, sleeping in the car or being in a drug treatment place.

I had entered 34 different treatment centers in 11 years. I was homeless and a junkie. I lied to all my friends. I took their money. I was a terrible person. I lied to the drug rehabs wanting to help me. I lied to the doctors. All I wanted was another fix. My arms were black and blue from the needles. I did not eat. I was a scary person. All I wanted was another bag of dope.

My trip to hell went on for 11 years. One day, I could not find any dope, so I decided to end my life. I took a needle and shot 30cc of bug spray and passed out. Someone saw me and called 911. When I woke up in the emergency room, I told them why I shot bug spray. I was sent to the Bellevue Hospital in New York City for 2 weeks. They released me, and I went back to Fulton Street and started all over again. On and on it went. I could not stop. The pain from not having was so bad. I was a broken man. All I wanted was to get a shot or die.

My dad cried, and my mom cried when I called and asked for money. Being loving parents, they sent money to me through Western Union. My sister cried, and so did my friends. They all wanted to see me get well. I did not care any longer. I wanted to die.

The last drug program I went to in upper Manhattan in the year 2000 sent me to Boca Raton, Florida. I finally broke the heroin habit after six hard months of pain and therapy. I was at the Boca House, a halfway house, working and doing well. But, I was not happy. I missed my wife and the children. She would not talk to me and would not let the kids talk to me. I missed the drugs. So, I went back to the pills after a year and partied in Boca, going to pill doctors and using the needle again until the bottom dropped out, and I lost everything again. I was homeless in South Florida. I lost a great job, and again, I was lost, hurt and scared.

My friend, Jeff, told me about Faith Farm in Fort Lauderdale. In August of 2001, he dropped me off, and he drove away. I have been at Faith Farm ever since.

After being at Faith Farm for 6 months, I dropped "dead" one day in front of the church. I was taken to Broward General and was in the ICU for two weeks before I came back to life. I was taken in for a major open-heart surgery with two valve replacements and a pacemaker put in my chest. I have Hepatitis C and have been testing for the possibility of having blood cancer.

I am now an employee of Faith Farm for the last 8 years. I have been drug free for more than 12 years. I have paid off $26,000 in past due child support. Mariel, my oldest daughter, has made me a grandfather. Although life has been a challenge, I now have Christ in my life. After all the above, I have finally found some peace.

Today, I know God loves me for He has kept me alive. He has a plan for me to help other men like myself to never use drugs again. I would like to thank everyone in my life for all your help, even when I was a lying person. I thank everyone here at Faith Farm for all your support. And thank you, Brother Dean, for believing in me.

William

First of all, I thank God for allowing me the opportunity to even be here, because in my eyes, I should be dead. I shouldn't even be allowed to live after the way I've acted for forty-eight years. I was being a mean person. I was a selfish person.

But one morning I woke up; and instead of picking up that bottle of liquor, I felt different for some reason. Instead of picking up that drink, I just got up and walked. I walked the streets for a couple of hours. Something had just come over me. I knew what it was, but I was trying to run from it. It was God. God had me under conviction. I knew in my heart what I was doing was wrong. He was talking to me. What really scared me the most was I had the feeling that this was it, and that there was no negotiating. It was either do it now or else. The next place was hell, because that's where I was headed.

On the bus ride down to Florida from Tennessee, I realized that I was hurt and broken, exhausted and completely at the "end of my rope." I was totally ready for a change and that change was to get to know God personally and to begin a relationship with Him. God was not a new concept for me. As a child I was raised in the church. I knew who God was. Although I knew about God, I didn't know Him personally. The only time I turned to God was when I was in trouble and looking for a way out. I figured I was hell-bound anyway.

After being at Faith Farm a few days, I started praying and reading my Bible. Eventually, I got this calmness about me that I'd never had. I had a different attitude about things and my outlook on life started changing. Soon, everyday became a good day, because it gave me an opportunity to do better than I did the day before. I found out quickly that it *ain't* about Bill. It *ain't got nothing* to do with me! I thought it was all me back in the days, but it's not. It's about Him and doing His will. Sometimes, throughout the day, I do wrong things, and I get mad. Sometimes I have smoke coming out of my ears. Around here, I get so mad, but the difference is I don't act on it. He reels me back in. There's one thing that I have learned since I've been here … that's trust in Him. He has gotten me to where I am today. I thank Him very much for that.

In closing, I would like to thank Faith Farm. I know it's not all about Faith Farm; but listen, Faith Farm taught me. They gave me the tools I needed to get my life straight and to become a better person. I would like to thank all my teachers for this one important thing—for obeying God's calling and being here for men like me who are hurting.

Thank you.

Raj

In fantasy and myth, homecoming is a dramatic event: bands play; the fatted calf is killed; a banquet prepared; and, there is rejoicing that the prodigal has returned. In reality, exile is frequently ended gradually, with no dramatic, external events to mark its passing. The haze in the air evaporates, and the world comes into focus; seeking gives way to finding; anxiety to satisfaction. Nothing is changed, and everything is changed.

My name is Raj, and I am from India. No, I have never owned any convenient stores or flea ridden cheap motels off Dixie Highway. And no, I wasn't the one who answered your call when you called for tech support. I am just here to tell you that addiction doesn't discriminate who you are, where you come from, how smart you are or how much money you've got.

My story is not any different than any other addict's. It's not important how I became an addict and how I lost everything, but what's important is how God saved me. After I lost everything, I had to move in with my brother, who is a doctor.

Every night, I came home high and got into an argument with my family. Every night, I promised them and myself that I was going to stop; and by morning, I was doing it all over again. Nobody in my family drank or used any kind of drugs, so they didn't know what to do with me; and, I didn't care. I had a death wish. Finally, the day came when my family couldn't take it anymore. They decided to put me in a program called "Cornerstone" at Wellington Regional Hospital.

It was Friday, and I was supposed to check into the program on Monday. That Saturday, my brother went to the hospital, since he was on a call and there was an emergency. While at work he started talking to this doctor about what was going on. This doctor, who was a Christian and had just returned from a missionary trip with Mike Brown, suggested that I should go to Faith Farm instead of Cornerstone. In fact, he would call Mike Brown and set everything up. My brother agreed. By Monday, I was at Faith Farm instead of Cornerstone. This was September 10, 1989.

Since I am from India and born in a Hindu family, I didn't know anything about Christianity or church. Because of that, people at Faith Farm thought I was not going to last more than a week. I felt people of Faith Farm needed more help than I did. They were nice, helpful and caring and probably phony, because nobody in their right mind is this happy. I just wanted to be here long enough to manipulate my family so I can go back and do what I was doing before. To survive spiritual giants at Faith Farm, I learned a couple of words like "Hallelujah" and "Praise God" … and it worked. They left me alone. My plan was to go on my first 8 hour pass after 30 days never to return.

The day came. It was Saturday, and I was excited to go home for good. My brother came to pick me up. He told me he needed to stop by the hospital. I said "OK" knowing he's a doctor. When we got there, I realized my father was in the hospital. A wound on his leg was not healing; and because he was a diabetic, they were talking about amputating his leg that Monday. My mom passed away when I was four years old, and my father raised me. He was my father and my mother. I tried to convince him that I should stay with him instead of going back to Faith Farm, but he insisted that I should go back and get the healing I needed.

At the end of the day, I was back at Faith Farm. I was sad and powerless. I wanted to help my dad but didn't know how. As I sat at the edge of my bed in the dorm, the guy who slept next to my bunk came and asked me about my pass. I told him what was going on and he said, "Why don't you pray." I wanted to kill him because I had heard that before, but I was desperate. So, I told him the truth ... that I didn't know how. He smiled and said he would pray with me; and he did. He told me to ask the pastor to pray for my father on Sunday, too. I did, and pastor prayed for my father, too. Surgery was on Monday.

On Wednesday, my brother came to see me. My first question to him was how did surgery go and how was my father doing? He told me that my father didn't have to go through the surgery, and he was recovering well. I couldn't believe what I was hearing. My brother is a doctor, and my sister-in-law is a doctor. They were both 99% sure about the surgery, but now he was saying that he didn't need it. My brother gave me some medical explanation, but I knew deep within my heart that God healed my father.

This was the day my life changed. I wanted to know this God. This is the God I wanted to serve forever. I ended up staying at Faith Farm for another four years until God opened up a door for me at Abiding Hearts. I ran that ministry for 16 years. And now, I am back again at Faith Farm for the last 5 years as a teacher to give back to the ministry that has saved my life.

I have been sober for 25 years, thanks to the grace of God and Faith Farm Ministries.

Author's note: Raj is an Intern who handles training for the Servant Leadership Service (SLS) students, which is an extended program after the basic 9 month program. Raj also handles the IT Department at the Boynton Beach campus. I have called Raj in my office at least three times and asked if we could hire him as an employee. He always defers, saying he is confident he is where the Lord wants him: As an Intern, giving back to Faith

Farm. This is the place where God reached him and delivered him from alcoholism. Raj is one of the most spiritual, Christian men I know, which is saying a lot considering his Hindu background.

Mikhail

I was born and raised in Russia. I got involved with the organized crime at the age of 14. I had everything I wanted—money, cars, women and drugs. If I wanted something, I got it. I thought I was happy. By the age of 18, I'd been stabbed, shot at twice and I was facing a long prison sentence. I wanted to get away from everything. My mom lived in Florida, so I decided to come to the United States. She helped me to get a Green Card.

In 2001, I moved to Florida to get a fresh start. I got a job and started to live a normal life. After a while, I gave up on the whole having a job idea and started selling drugs. I was back to what I knew best—women, drugs, and going out to live in the "fast lane." I had everything, but I was miserable. During these years, I've totaled a few cars, got two DUIs and other numerous arrests. I finally got arrested for trafficking cocaine. By having a good lawyer, my charges were lessened to a possession charge. I was sentenced to the Palm Beach County Sheriff's Drug Farm, followed by a halfway house and a few years of probation.

While on probation, I went to the doctor and got roxys, xanax and somas. I was using and my probation could not violate me. I quit my job because I was making more money selling drugs. My last girlfriend left me because she was scared for her life. She didn't know who was going to come through the door—cops, feds or someone to rob or kill us. My life was out of control. I was living in hotels. I was depressed and tired of life. Because of the things I've done, I was trying to kill myself by shooting large amounts of pills, crack and powder cocaine. I could not stand the person I'd become.

Psalm 120:6 states,

My soul has dwelt too long with one who hates peace.

I was desperate. I came to Faith Farm because I wanted to change. Since being here, I found out who God is and developed a relationship with Him. I started to read the Bible and realized that I broke all of God's commandments. I now know that I was addicted to sin. I got baptized and accepted Jesus Christ as my Lord and Savior. Now I live in peace with myself. Revelation 3:20 states,

Behold, I stand at the door and knock. If anyone hears my voice and opens the door, I will come in to him and dine with him, and him with Me.

Thank you.

Joni

"Let the words of my mouth and the meditation of my heart be acceptable in your sight, oh Lord, my strength and my redeemer."

I was born in Charlotte, North Carolina, and I was raised in a Christian, church-going family. My paternal grandfather was a Southern Primitive Baptist preacher. My family attended every Sunday and Wednesday church service. My mother taught Sunday school; my father was a deacon, and my sister and I were involved in all of the children and youth ministries. I was baptized for the first time at the age of 7 years.

I was always the overweight, chunky kid with self-esteem issues. I was called fat so much that I came to believe it and proved it to be true. I was an excellent student. But, I was also somewhat mischievous.

In the 4th grade, I advocated for a girls' basketball program at my elementary school. One was started, and I began playing competitive, organized basketball for the next 10 years.

I started drinking and experimenting with drugs at the age of 15. By the age of 18, I was drinking to intoxication every weekend. At the time, I didn't think this was a problem, as everyone I hung around with was drinking. I finally fit in, or so I thought. Everyone liked me and invited me to their parties because I was the life of the party, and I was obviously extremely entertaining.

I began getting into trouble at school because of my behavior. I was dismissed from the basketball team and suspended from school during my sophomore year because of drinking on the bus on the way home from a basketball game. During my senior year, I quit school and moved to live with my aunt and uncle in order to complete high school. I have been in many different colleges, many different times, but have yet to earn a degree.

I experimented with many drugs over the years ... trying anything that was put in front of me, but the only thing that ensnared me was alcohol. At the age of 19, I obtained an entry-level position with a large financial institution; and over the next 20 years, I had a very successful and lucrative career.

I continued partying and drinking excessively and was charged with my first DUI at the age of 25. This was my life for many years; working all week, partying all weekend, having fair-weather friends, disposable boyfriends and relationships of no substance. I covered my loneliness and pain with alcohol and food.

In 2000, at the age of 30, I decided that it was time to get married, so I married the first man who was willing. Sadly, we did not take the time to get to know one another. He was an abusive man, and I was drinking in excess. The marriage lasted for 6 months and we divorced. Within the next year, I met and married my second husband.

In 2004, I was diagnosed as possibly being bipolar and was sent to a psychiatrist. This doctor questioned my drinking habits, and his diagnosis rendered me an alcoholic. The next day, I began a 16-week outpatient recovery program and remained sober for almost 5 years.

During this time, I was eating excessively, and my weight was spiraling out of control. In 2007, I had surgery to correct my weight problem. However, the surgery did not fix the unresolved issues on the inside of me.

I Samuel 16:7 says,

Do not look at his appearance or at his physical stature, because I have refused him. For the Lord does not see as man sees; for man looks at the outward appearance, but the Lord looks at the heart.

At this point in my career, I was Corporate Vice President of Technology and Operations, managing a staff of more than one hundred, with a six-figure salary. I was offered a position in the greater New York City area with a significant salary increase. My husband and I mutually decided that we would accept this offer and relocate to New Jersey. After I began the transition and relocation process, my husband decided that he did not want to move. Our marital problems intensified, so we separated and eventually divorced. I was lonely and misguided, and I relapsed. I moved to New Jersey by myself, which began a tumultuous, three-year suicidal binge. During all of this, I never once sought God.

In August 2009, I came to South Florida for 21 days to a secular rehab program. My sobriety lasted for 5 days. My plans obviously were not working out as I had hoped in the Northeast, so I made the decision to move back to North Carolina. I thought that living in North Carolina, being close to my family and friends, attending church and being re-baptized would help me to overcome alcohol. This was not an accurate assessment.

In November of that year in New Jersey, I drove head-on into a utility pole and was charged with my second DUI. In North Carolina in May 2010, I was charged with another DUI. Fortunately for me, circumstances were such that this DUI was dismissed. By the grace of God, I did not hurt or kill anyone or myself.

In spite of all of this, I continued drinking. In August 2010, I came back to South Florida to re-enter the same rehab center. This time, I stayed for the complete program. They told me that I had to make a life change; so I packed my belongings, quit my job, and moved to Delray Beach. My sobriety was short-lived. In July of 2011, I relapsed and found myself on a horrific spiral into hell. I was so broken and empty inside that all I wanted to do was to die. Alcohol was once again consuming my life.

At this point, it seemed that everyone around me began speaking Faith Farm into my life. In August 2012, I was terminated from my job for calling in sick too often. This caused me to pick up the phone and call Faith Farm. I was accepted into the program and arrived here on August 30, 2012.

When I came to Faith Farm, I was completely broken and hopeless. I felt utterly worthless and lost. I cried all day, every day, for several weeks. All I could think was that I had been given so much. How did my life end up like this? I now know that I was seeking all the wrong things. Money, men and material possessions could not fill the void in my soul. Colossians 3:2 says,

> Set your mind on the things above, not on the things on
> the earth.

Having lived in my iniquities for more than 25 years, I proclaim that I have been delivered from my past lifestyle choices, including smoking and my dependence on antidepressants. Today, I am on no medication other than the Word of God.

I now believe that when you commit your life to the Lord and walk in obedience to Him, He will restore you from the inside out. I no longer believe Satan's lies.

Psalm 71:20 says,

> *You, who have shown me great and severe troubles,*
> *shall revive me again, and bring me up again from the*
> *depths of the earth.*

Through my daily walk here at Faith Farm, my quiet time of Bible reading, prayer and meditation, praise and worship, along with my classes, I now know the truth. John 8:32 states,

> *And you shall know the truth, and the truth shall make*
> *you free.*

"Alcohol" does not define me; "weight" does not define me; "unworthy" does not define me. I am a beautiful child of God, our King, which makes me a princess. I am worthy of everything that God has promised me. I am filled with faith that He will guide me in the right direction, and I have hope for a future beyond anything I could have ever imagined for myself. Today, I am truly free.

God will give you the desires of your heart, but through the transformation of your mind, God will change your desires to match His. Matthew 6:33 says,

> *Seek first the kingdom of God and his righteousness,*
> *and all these things will be added to you. (NASB)*

He has restored my hope, my faith and the ability to love myself and others. God has done for me what I could not do for myself.

Today, there is nothing more I want than to fulfill His will and purpose for my life and to serve Him in everything that I do. I am not perfect, but my goal is to be more like Jesus Christ, my Lord and Savior, each and every day.

Author's Note: *Joni is a poised, sophisticated lady, who stayed after graduation to become an Intern at Faith Farm. Joni has been acting as Assistant to the Executive Director, and is responsible for much of the typewritten testimonies in this book, transcribing them from audio recordings. Joni is truly a transformed person.*

One day at lunch, I was sitting in a group, which included Joni. I mentioned to her that recently I didn't even recognize the arresting photo of one of the other women in the program. She was so beautiful the first time I saw her, which is after she was in the program for five months. She looked nothing like her booking photo. Joni said, "Did you ever see my intake photo?" I said, "No."

She took her phone, scrolled through the photos and handed her phone to me. I looked at the image and then looked up at her. I looked back to the phone image and back up to her again, and said, "This couldn't be you." She assured me it was her. My eyes became full of tears, and I wanted to cry. It looked nothing like Joni... not even close enough to recognize. I had been shown intake pictures of men before and found them unrecognizable. But I was not used to seeing pictures of the women in the program. Joni was a thoroughly changed person, inside and out. She had gone through a physical and spiritual metamorphosis at Faith Farm.

Carlos

I was born in Puerto Rico, June 22, 1955. At the age of 2, my parents, already married for 4 years, decided to get a divorce. Why? I do not know. So, at 2 years old, my 24-year-old father and I moved to New York with his 2 sisters living in the Bronx. It wasn't easy for us. It was difficult for my father to find work. However, after 6 months, my father landed a job making furniture for a company and worked in conjunction with the armed forces. At the very same time, my father met a woman. She lived in the same apartment building, and she was also divorced with 3 children of her own. They started dating and eventually got married.

So here I was; almost 5 years old with a new mom, 2 brothers and a sister. After a couple of years went by, my father won custody of me from my (biological) mother. This is when things started changing.

My father worked long hours, so I spent most of the time with my step-family. The next 10 years were hell. I was being abused sexually, verbally and mentally. I was looking for an escape. By the time I reached the age of 14, I found my escape on the streets of the South Bronx with gangs and drugs on every corner. I started smoking pot and stopped going to school. I got held back in the 8th grade. After that, I got smart and made it into high school, Alfred E. Smith High.

I was still spending most of my time in the streets with my friends, smoking every day. I was able to graduate in 1974. I spent that summer in the Bronx. I got an opportunity for a job in New Brunswick, New Jersey, working for Rutgers University, managing 3 dormitories that housed over 500 students. I bought my first car and was doing very well for a few years.

I found myself missing the streets of the Bronx, so I would drive to New York every weekend. One day there was a big cut back in the state of New Jersey, and I got laid off. I lived on unemployment for about a year and finally moved back to New York. I moved in with a friend of mine, who at the time was dealing heroin. Within a month, I was shooting up, and I never looked back.

For the next 30 years, heroin became everything to me. I began selling, and yes, I made a lot of money. However, what I made I spent on drugs. Romans 6:21 says this:

> *What fruit did you have then in the things of which you*
> *are now ashamed? For the end of those things is death.*

My addiction took off like a bird in flight. Drugs and alcohol became a way of life, like eating and taking a bath. Everything that was important became unimportant. My addiction had become powerful and insidious. It knew me better than I knew myself. It took me to places I didn't want to go. It made me do things I didn't want to do. I could not see the light; I was blind.

While using, I lived in another world. I experienced brief jolts of reality and self-awareness. It seemed that I was two different people ... Dr. Jekyll and Mr. Hyde. I tried to get my life together before my next run. Sometimes I could do this very well, but later it was less important and more impossible. In the end, Mr. Hyde took over.

The book of Narcotics Anonymous speaks of jails, institutions and death. I did the institutions and jails many, many times, but why not death? Death, I thought, was my only way out of this life of pain and misery. I tell you why not death. It was because of God!

John 3:16 says this:

For God so loved the world that He gave His only begotten Son, that whoever believes in Him should not perish, but have everlasting life.

When I read that verse, I felt something very profound happen. I couldn't exactly put my finger on it. Today, I believe God reached down and touched me. Sometimes in life, what appears to be the end is really a new beginning.

I often prayed when I was hurting; and now, I find myself praying regularly and not hurting as often or as intensely. I know praying is asking for help and meditation is listening for God's answer.

I have been ordained by God to be here, where I can finally say enough is enough and to break the chains that bonded me. I am free. God heard my prayers. Peace to you all who are in Christ.

Troy

Author's Note: Troy came through the Program and excelled at everything he did. He displayed a particular skill for a sense of style in furniture and became the buyer for new furniture for resale. His "eye" for trends in furniture allowed the Boynton Beach campus store to become one of the larger Ashley Furniture dealers in South Florida. Troy has held several positions, working up to Assistant Director and finally Director of the Boynton Beach Faith Farm campus. Troy is a great manager of people and things, and he is responsible for over 60% of all Faith Farm, micro-business enterprises income. He is a very valuable asset to Faith Farm.

I started using drugs when I was seventeen years old. I started out smoking pot. I didn't use any hard drugs until I got to college in 1979, and I started snorting cocaine with buddies. It progressed from pot to cocaine to crack cocaine. About the time I started smoking crack was when it hit the scenes real hard. Crack cocaine is what really brought me down in life.

When I look back, one of the reasons I got out of control was failure. Every time I turned around, I was failing at something: school; professional career; basketball; career in the Navy; marriages; everything I did, I failed. And the more I failed, the worse my using became to hide my pain.

I've always loved sports and athletics. That was my escape. That was how I escaped from things like adultery, drugs and being physically abused. But later in life, I found out that I became those people. I became an adulterer and a drug addict. What I saw, I became; except I never put my hands on a woman. I never went down that road. That was the one thing I said I would never do. It was very scary for me to see my stepfather physically beat my mother. I would try to intervene, and he would smack me down. It was very painful. But looking back on my childhood, everything that I saw, I became.

I was always very good in sports, and I got a scholarship to college. Everything that God gave me, it seemed like I blew it, including that scholarship. I was fortunate that I was good enough, and they wanted me overseas to play ball. I thank God for that. But, I couldn't stay sober over there, and they kicked me out of the league.

I got back home with the money that I had made, and I blew $200,000 in about six or seven months. My wife left me. It was a hard time. I was lonely, and I had nothing or nobody. Basically, I had become what my environment was. The one thing that was missing, I found out, was church. I never went to church. I never had God in my life, and it wasn't until I decided that I was going to put God in my life that things turned around for me. I'm just grateful that God pulled me out of the mirey muck I was in and set my feet on a rock to stay. It's been a hard life. To look at me, you wouldn't think that my life took that turn, but it did.

I remember one of the most painful things was my marriage breaking up. When my daughter was about two years old, my wife joined the Air Force without me knowing. When I found out that she had joined the Air Force, I said to her, "Why didn't you tell me?" She said, "Somebody had to do something; you're using drugs." She was working part-time and living with her parents. I was not working; I was draining our bank accounts, using drugs, and it was a real ugly scene. So, she decided to join the Air Force, just to get us out of her parents' house. She said, "You know, me, you and the baby—we can leave and start a life of our own."

Well, my wife got through basic training. When she came home, she decided that she didn't want to be married anymore. That was a blow to me, because the whole time she was gone, I was trying real hard to turn things around with my life so that we could have a life together. Her asking for a divorce was really, really crushing to me. After spending all that time taking care of my daughter and trying to get my life back on track, it was really a heartfelt blow. So, I decided I was going to join the Navy Reserves. That's what I did for a little while, just to help myself make some money and kind of keep my life going.

After we divorced, I moved back home to West Palm Beach with my mother. The area that she lived in was very drug infested. I hadn't been a hardcore user until I moved back to that neighborhood. The more I felt self-pity for myself, the more I sunk into using crack cocaine. I just couldn't find a way out. I was living on the streets for a while. Nobody wanted anything to do with me. I started stealing and robbing. I was not to be trusted at this time. I was living with my grandfather and I was stealing from him, but he didn't care. He loved me unconditionally. He didn't care what I did. He loved me enough to see me through. It wasn't until he passed that I realized I needed to turn my life around. There was nobody else who was going to love me unconditionally like he did. He passed in November of 1997, and I came to Faith Farm in February of 1998.

When I got to Faith Farm, I just thought that I was going to get off drugs and try to lead a normal life. I had no idea that God had a plan for me to stay here and to work in the ministry. But, after getting sober and clean for a while, things started coming back to me. I cleaned myself up and started thinking clearly like the man I was supposed to be. I started working in the thrift store, and my talents started evolving as I was in the store. I loved selling furniture; I loved the people, and I loved the customers. It was just something that I really loved to do, and I was serving God. I never once thought that I would become Assistant Director or Director in this program. I just figured I would get off drugs and go back home. But God has really, really blessed me. I have a wife and a son. He's given me all of my family back. He's given me so much more than I thought I could have ever attained.

While here at Faith Farm, I've tried to figure out why my life took the turn that it did. Looking back, I can remember the class called "Houses" here at Faith Farm. That's when my eyes were really opened to one of the reasons why I did what I did. I found out that it stemmed from when I was about 12 years old and my mother was in an adulterous relationship. One night I caught her with a man in a sex act. The pastor believed that scarred me for life, and now that I look back on it, it did bother me. I had never seen anything like that. I knew nothing about sex at 12 years old. It really baffled me that my mother was sleeping with another man while she was married. I believe I've had some trust issues because of that. My mother's husband used to beat me when I was younger. I was abused, not sexually, but physically. It was painful. When I look back on my childhood, it was a sad childhood. My mother had eight kids and each one of us had different fathers. Out of eight kids, every one of my brothers and sisters knew their father, except for me. It was a tough household to grow up in. But, I always wanted better for myself.

While I've been here at Faith Farm, God has done nothing but bless me and put me in the right situations. I've never asked for an application for a job or a promotion. Every position at Faith Farm that I've had, I was asked to take; and I take that as a blessing from God. That's not bragging, it's just the way that God had it played out. God has put some good people in front of me, like Brother Dean. I've always looked up to him. He's been the father that I thought I should have had. At fifty-two years old, I don't know my father. I've never met him to this day. If he walked in the room right now, I wouldn't know who he was, and he is still living today.

You don't have to think about all the bad things that happen in your life when you're using drugs. But now, when I think about some of the things I've been through in life (like using drugs), and how painful it was, it just takes my mind somewhere else. I just thank God that He pulled me in at the right time. He didn't leave me out there to suffer, because it is so painful when you're "ripping and running" trying to find drugs to stay high. It doesn't work. Drugs are not the answer to hide your pain.

So, thank God. Thank God for Faith Farm.

Sara

Good morning. St Francis of Assisi once said, "Preach the Gospel daily. Use words."

Let us pray. Lord, may my testimony make a difference for you who are disproportionate to whom I am. Our God is Lord of change. Change is an inevitable part of life. We cannot avoid fiery trials. God will overrule and work through tragedies to accomplish His purpose for those who respond to His call. Changes in life are cause to remember that God is faithful; yesterday, today and forever. Amen.

Nine months ago, I checked my bags at the Phoenix airport and boarded a Delta flight bound for West Palm Beach—final destination, Faith Farm. Most Phoenix locals are familiar with the ancient Egyptian mythical creature it's named after: A beautiful, long bird soaring high above the Arabian Desert for five or six hundred years, consumed itself in the fire and rising out of the ashes, a new creature. Flying at 33,000 feet, I reflected on how my life resembled the mythical Phoenix. Raised in a good Christian home, active in my youth group, the most trouble I got into, and I'm sorry to say, Becky, you were with me; was toilet papering the pasture cows. It was bad the next day ... it rained. That's why they locked up the toilet paper.

By 18, I married my high school sweetheart and went to college full time. I became an adult in that relationship, lending my attitudes and framing my values. For 22 years, I linked my whole life around my husband by a thousand threads, and suddenly I found those threads snapped into a million pieces and found myself wondering who I am.

Ladies, when we place God-like expectations on our men, and we expect them to make up for what's likely missing inside of us, we can't help but be disappointed. I was devastated that my marriage ended. Loss consumed me like a tsunami. I made making a living more important than a living God. I felt safe because of my mutual funds and my level of income. Rather than allowing God's hands to hold mine, I sacrificed my time and energy at the altar of material gain.

At "40 Something," I was suddenly single. I was enjoying solitude but feared being alone. So, I did what most suddenly single women do. I went shopping … on a manhunt. Just keeping it real!

I met a wealthy, attractive man who had it all; Atheism added. I believed the lie that it was my responsibility to change him. I entered into this relationship which quickly turned violent, bringing me to a place I thought I'd never be. The restraining order seemingly had no effect on him. For 4 years, I ran from state to state from him with a bag of disappointment, a trunk load of fear, an overnight bag of loneliness, a carry-on of abandonment and a makeup case to cover my guilt and shame; only to return to my abuse of chardonnay as my closest companion.

One morning, I sped away on my Vespa. Traveling at 40 miles per hour, I had a head-on collision with an SUV. Both vehicles were totaled; my Vespa and I lodged under the SUV. Miraculously, no one in the SUV was injured. I was rushed via ambulance to the emergency room with serious injuries. God had spared my life once again. Shortly thereafter, I quit my job; packed, got in my truck and in the darkness, made my contingency plans in my mind. I had nowhere to go except for a shelter for battered women, and I didn't want to do that again. I cried out to God: "When will you?" and "If only!" I realized then that if I tried to move on my own strength and not by faith, this cycle of abuse would continue, and I would have certainly died. God answered my cry. He didn't speak to me dramatically as he did with

Moses through a burning bush. He came to me in a calm stillness and whispered, "When you trust me … When you obey me!"

He led me to a Godly woman named Gereda—a woman of action, not platitudes, empty prayers and condolences. Gereda took me into her home; and together we called my sister, Becky, who for the past 5 years prayed endlessly on her hands and knees for protection of my life. Together, they made it possible for me to come to Faith Farm.

Here at Faith Farm, those years in the making were so quickly destroyed. God took the ashes and made beauty out of it. I learned how to live a lifestyle of service and relentless pursuit of holiness. I learned to respond rather than react and to guard my tongue. He slowed the anger and was quick to forgive. Jesus said we shouldn't let our hearts be afraid. He promised "a peace that passes understanding;" a peace that comes in the midst of trials. He alone is my safety and my security, and I shouldn't put my trust in people, places and things, as I have in the past. I began to experience peace by being still and content with whatever circumstances I incurred here at Faith Farm. And, the baggage that I carry around on the carousel of my mind; Sister Diane and I packed that baggage and sent it on a plane to Japan. God allows me, from time to time, to re-experience varying degrees of the pain that's stored in my memory. The old scars begin to pinch.

My Christianity does not alter or erase the facts of my past. It alters my perspective of the facts. Dressed with the "Armor of God," I'm able to move forward with courage in greater victory and wholeness. No longer a spiritual nomad or wandering Phoenix; today, I'm a person of purpose and destiny. By accepting Christ, our lives and our minds change to the reality of redemption by which we are healed; no longer bound by fear, no longer chained to our past and its shame. We are free … free to capture the vision of His mercy, to catch a glimpse of His beauty; renewing us and changing us in His all-consuming fire; creating new creatures out of the ashes. Last March, I was commissioned with a prophetic word that I would take my message elsewhere. I leave tomorrow to start that journey in Ecuador to serve God with my sister, Becky. There are moments when I think I'm inadequate for the mission field. Then Jesus whispers these words to me: "In weakness, there is My strength."

Author's Note: *Sara's sister, Becky, flew in from her mission in Ecuador to attend her sister's Faith Farm graduation. Sara then returned to Ecuador with Becky to serve in the mission field as well.*

Timothy

My early years involved great experiences with the Lord and in the faith. My parents raised me in the ministry as they went to Bible College, attended multiple missionary journeys and pastored a church. I learned much about how a Christian man should walk through my father, as he supported our primarily homeless congregation through his profession as a CPA. Despite my upbringing, I went through the majority of my youth without the ability to fit in with my peers. Because of this, I turned to drug use in order to gain and maintain friendships and a sense of belonging. This changed for a time when I started turning my life and will back over to Christ's care and control.

I met a woman. I was convinced I would spend the rest of my life with her and quickly married her. I have 2 sons with her, whom God has used mightily in my life and many times saved me from myself. To make a long story short, everything fell apart in the marriage; and I found myself at Faith Farm, while pursuing a certificate of divorce on the grounds of marital infidelity. I chose to leave 4 weeks before graduation as she had fled the state, leaving my children with my parents. I recall sitting in the audience at what would have been my own graduation. I was still totally broken and had not completely surrendered to God. One thing I did that day was give her back over to the Lord as I placed my wedding ring in the offering basket during the service.

I would spend the next year trying to get my life back together without really confronting my sin. This is where my will and my path led me: sitting for sixty days in county jail, and facing state prison for breaking into my own parents' home. I kidnapped the son my parents knew and made him susceptible to every kind of demonic influence imaginable. Due to a classification error, I found myself in a maximum security cell.

I called out to God for protection and provision and He came through in a most provident way. Within three weeks, daily weapon searches and cage matches became Bible studies and worship services. The whole atmosphere in that place had changed from darkness to light. "The peace of God which surpasses all understanding" took over. God proved to me that He was my protector and provider. After this experience, I recommitted my life to God and the call of the ministry I had received at a young age. He gave me two scriptures in response to this commitment. Romans 11:22 says,

> *Therefore, consider the goodness and severity of God on those who fell, severity, but toward you, goodness, if you continue in his goodness. Otherwise, you also will be cut off.* (NKJV)

The second one was Ephesians 4:28, which reads,

> *But him who stole, steal no longer, but rather let him labor, working with his hands what is good, that he may have something to give to him who has need.* (NKJV)

Soon after this, I was admitted to Faith Farm and was assured of a year or more prison sentence as part of a plea agreement. Once again, God proved to me that:

> *All things work together for the good of those who love Him and are called according to His purpose.* (NKJV)

At the last minute, the plea was changed to have me attend Dunklin Memorial Camp in place of a prison sentence. However, God and his providence saw fit for me to be at Faith Farm. With a mighty hand and outstretched arm, He sent confusion into the courtroom, and the end result was that I was able to remain and complete Faith Farm in place of Dunklin. Psalm 34:19 states,

> *Many are the afflictions of the righteous but the Lord*
> *delivers them out of them all.* NKJV)

Being here this time around, I have experienced the inner healing required to mend the wounds left by an adulterous spouse, and to get through the bitterness that sprouted after I burned out and walked away from the ministry. I've been able to begin to give my life and my will over to Christ's care and control, working side by side with the Holy Spirit as He shines the light on the character defects and sin in my life and gently helps me take the steps necessary to put an end to it. I've come to the conclusion, while here at Faith Farm, that for years I had been living in deception; having a form of Godliness, but denying the power thereof. Professing myself to be wise, I became one of the fools. My foolishness in sin had overtaken me.

The Scripture that has come to characterize my time here, and will do well in finalizing this speech, would have to be 2 Corinthians 7:10-11. It says,

> *For Godly sorrow produces repentance, which leads to*
> *salvation, not to be regretted. But the sorrow of the*
> *world produces death. Observe this very thing: that*
> *you sorrowed in a Godly manner; what diligence it*
> *produced in you; what clearing of yourselves; what*
> *indignation; what fear; what vehement desire; what*
> *seal of vindication. In all things, you proved yourself to*
> *be clear in this manner.* (NKJV)

81

I pray those of you who have heard my voice but haven't come to a personal, saving knowledge of Jesus Christ, begin to turn your life and will over to His care and control. I must warn you that the Christian life is not all cake and balloons, but it is power.

I'd like to thank all the staff and teachers at Faith Farm for all your time, guidance, direction, and everything that you've provided. You're helping a lot of people. I would also be remiss if I didn't mention Celebrate Recovery. These meetings were the catalyst and the wake-up call for me to begin dealing with the real issues that landed me here. I appreciate everyone involved in Celebrate Recovery that really helped me out with issues I wasn't able to face on my own. I'm not supposed to mention people specifically, but I'm going to do it anyway. I won't say your name because you asked me not to, but I believe it was a divine appointment working under you. You've been a mentor and a friend to me, and I cherish you. There are better days ahead.

Thank you!

Author's Note: *Tim is one who came through Faith Farm a second time. Since this is a volunteer program, some walk out and don't complete the program, as Tim did. However, the second time, he "got it" and is truly a changed man. Sometimes, attending Faith Farm is a great motivator, in lieu of incarceration and serving out a prison sentence.*

Nancy

I fell in love with Jesus when I was a small child. I was raised in a loving, Christian home with Christian values. I was baptized when I was 9 years old.

Before high school, we moved and my family stopped going to church on a regular basis. I changed high schools 6 times. I finally gave up on school. I quit and never finished. In the past, on applications for jobs, I would lie about completing high school. Anytime a promotion would be offered, I would turn it down if further education was required. I would like to thank Faith Farm for giving me the opportunity to prepare for and take the GED test. I completed the test on May 5th, so thank you, Faith Farm.

I was married very young and had 3 children. When my youngest daughter was about 4, a neighbor asked me to go to church with her. My family and I started going to church. I found myself being drawn to rededicate my life to the Lord. I wanted to, but I also still wanted to party. I wanted to be a Christian my way, and I was not reading the Handbook. I would go to Bible study on Wednesday nights, Sunday services, and church events. Then I would go home and live as if I didn't even know Jesus.

I raised my kids in a state of reckless chaos much of the time. Drugs and alcohol were part of my life, both recreationally and because of medical issues. I don't know how to explain that my children still love me and want the best for me after everything I've done, except to say that God is a merciful God.

For years before I came to Faith Farm, I knew I needed God's help but I didn't ask. I experienced several life-changing losses in the midst of, and mostly due to, my addictions. I was running from life and all the shame and pain I had caused my family. I ran to Arizona, where my sister lives. I thought I would just start over. My nephew drove me to Tucson.

I got a job at the TTT Truck Stop in Tucson. I started putting some money in the bank, and I began to feel as if I might have a future after all. That is when I met Tony. We became friends. Tony suggested we go to church. We talked about God and our church experiences, and we decided to find a church that would fit both of us.

After a couple of job changes, we ended up in North Port, Florida. We bought a house, and Tony asked me to marry him. I knew I had a problem that I could not take into another marriage. I knew I loved Tony. I also knew he deserved better than what I had to offer him at the time. Therefore, I tried to sabotage our relationship. Tony continued to pray for me and never gave up on us. We also continued to go to church. The time we spent together was increasingly stressful.

I remember one Sunday going to the altar and crying out to God. I told Him to take my life. I was not surrendering to God. I was giving up on life. I remember a woman praying with me. I went back to my seat; and a minute later, a man from our church named Peter sat next to me. After a conversation with Peter, I started going to an Overcomers group that he conducted at our church. I was going to the meetings at church and AA meetings, but I was still drinking, and I baker-acted myself twice (committed to a mental health treatment facility for evaluation).

Peter's wife, Lana, gave me information about Faith Farm. I called and spoke to a woman, whom I now know as Sister Paula. She said there was no room, but that she would put me on the waiting list. I hung up, went to the liquor store, and got a bottle. I called again, desperate and asked, "How long is that waiting list?" I really needed to go somewhere!

On September 14, Sister Paula called and told me there was an opening. Then, I was undecided! She said, "You need to make a decision and call by tomorrow, or I'll have to give the bed to someone who needs it." The next day was my birthday, and we all know what I wanted to do for my birthday. I begged her not to give that bed away. "I'll call you tomorrow," I said.

Now, I was faced with the answer to my prayer, and I was so uncomfortable. I didn't know what to do. Tony and I talked. I talked to my sisters and my kids. Everyone was excited for me ... except me. I kept saying to everyone, "Tony and I can't even talk to each other for seven months." Everyone was OK with that, except me! They said, "It'll go by fast; you'll see." So, Tony brought me to Faith Farm on September 18, 2010.

To say I was less than grateful at first would be an understatement. However, after being faced with "straighten up or go home," I knew I had to stay. I also knew that I wanted Tony to be a part of my recovery, because he was my friend and my encourager. I got into a bit of trouble (calling Tony on a field trip) and that earned me a trip to the Director's office. I was so ashamed of myself, but I explained how much Tony and I love each other and how good he is for me. So, Sister Ann said, "If he loves you so much, tell him to prove it. If he loves you, ask him to marry you! If he doesn't, you'll know where you stand. If he does, we can have the wedding here. "

I walked out of the office faced with the fact that I had to ask Tony to marry me and take a chance on him saying no. I was scared. Do you know how slow the mail is when you are waiting for the answer to an important question?

It was a "Big Sale" Saturday. I was working in the clothing room and Sister Paula asked me to come with her. Uh oh! I thought I was in trouble. She told me to sit on the golf cart. She got on, and she took my hand and said, "Tony told me to tell you yes, yes, yes, yes!" So, Sister Paula proposed to me. Then I remember her saying, "Do you want to go tell Sister Ann, 'I told you so?'"

We got married in this church on November 23rd. Pastor Jim and Sister Debbie counseled us, and then Pastor Jim conducted the service. My son, Zack, gave me away and my daughter, Lisa, stood up with me.

Since we've been married, Tony has been to every Sunday service, and he has been such a part of this healing experience. We have even teased about him being a student here, out on work release. I learned to put God before everything, including my marriage. I could have gone home. I could have not finished. That would have been the easy thing to do. However, I knew I still had some changes in my heart to deal with. Jesus was not finished with me. I was tired of wandering around and around that mountain. Enough is enough! I was done!

Little did I know I had just begun a completely new level of relationship with Jesus! The day I started really walking in faith and totally surrendering to God, I literally was so full of peace that I felt as if I would burst. I claimed this verse: Philippians 4:6-7, which says,

> Do not worry about anything, but in everything, by prayer and supplication with thanks giving, let your requests be made known to God. And the peace of God, which surpasses all understanding, will guard your heart and your mind. (NIV)

That word, supplication, means "earnestly seeking."

I went so far as to tack this verse to the underside of my bunk. Everyday got a little bit easier. Big things would come up, changes would happen. I was riding the wings of the Holy Spirit. Everything that came against me, and there were many, I gave to God. But, each time it got easier. I am excited about my future, but I have no preconceived notions that the next part of my life's journey will be easy. In fact, God promises that trials will come; but He will never leave me or forsake me, if I seek Him. Whatever is in my future, I pray I will always do it unto the glory of God.

I would like to thank Pastor Jim and Sister Debbie. Your authentic passion for this ministry is the shining example of Jesus that this world needs. God Bless you both.

I would like to thank God for the staff of the women's program. I will always cherish the words that you have spoken into my life. And thanks to my sisters in Christ. Due to our unique connection to God and each other, we will meet again!

Bambi

Once Upon A time
A Fairy Tale written by Bambi

Once upon a time, a woman *(me),* whose name is Bambi, had two lovely children; a girl and a boy; and a husband who provided for them. In 2000, there was an empty spot in my heart. With an empty nest, I sought to see if the grass was greener on the other side. I became out of control and I separated from my family. I loved the life of not having to explain my whereabouts or doings.

As that year went on, I still felt that emptiness inside. In the meantime, my family wanted an explanation for my behavior. I really did not have an explanation. I told them I raised my family properly; now it was time for Bambi to see what her life could really be like. Since I married at an early age, with an independent attitude and my addiction flaring, I went from proper to out of control.

In 2005 on Mother's Day, my husband served me with divorce papers, and we did divorce. I did not think it could go that far. That's not the Mother's Day gift I was expecting. I was lonely and I felt as though I had lost my best friend. I dove deeper into my addiction.

Holding a job for sixteen years at a Honda plant, I was fired for my lack of attendance. Still, I had that attitude: Oh well, I have a 401(k), and I can find another job. Well, it is not as easy as one may think; two part time jobs, and very little of the 401(k) left. Needless to say, I was heading for disaster, turning away from my family who cared while watching me fall. My family wanted to help, but my attitude got in the way. Once again, I shut them out, and I was slipping away from reality.

In 2008, I thought my life was over. I had lost my best friend in a jet-ski accident. Yes! My husband of 25 years of marriage was now gone.

At this time in my life, that once green grass had turned to brown.

In the next two years, I had no concerns in the world...so I thought. I did not care about life anymore. John 3:20 states,

> Everyone who does evil hates the light for fear that his deeds will be exposed.

James 1:8 pointed to the fact that I had become ...

> A doubled-minded woman, unstable in all I did.

November 2011, my daughter came to me stating that she was willing to give me another chance to get my life back together. She would take care of all the expenses for me to seek help for my addiction. She just wanted her mother back in her life; not the one with an addiction. I had already hit rock bottom with no money left; no job, eating meals on wheels and about to lose my home. There had to be a change in my life, because my way was not working.

The day after Thanksgiving, I said my good-byes and headed to Florida for rehab. I followed all the rules in my classes to help with my addiction. When I was finished with rehab, I still felt that emptiness inside. I had a talk with my roommate. She had convinced me that instead of AA meetings, I should try a CR meeting. I said, "What?" She said it was a Christian based recovery...Celebrate Recovery.

I grew up knowing who God was, but did not have that personal faith. So I said, "Why not? What do I have to lose?" Celebrate Recovery meetings were held at Faith Farm; and as soon I stepped foot on the grounds of Faith Farm, I knew this was the right place for me. I had denied Christ in my heart too long.

I came into the program in February 2012. I knew then that it was God that I was missing. Isaiah 54:4-8 says,

> *Do not fear, for you will not be ashamed; neither be disgraced, for you will not be put to shame; For you will forget the shame of your youth. And will not remember the reproach of your widowhood anymore. For your maker is your husband, The Lord of hosts is His name: And your Redeemer is the Holy one of Israel.*

I found my Prince charming…. Jesus Christ.

The End! But it is just the beginning.

God Bless.

I want to thank my daughter, Nicole, for coming all the way from Ohio. Please forgive me all the hurts and wrong doing to cause pain in your life and family, and to all my family that could not attend. I Love You All.

MAMA'S   BACK !!!!!!!!!!!!!!!!!

Fred

My name is Fred. I was born in Harlem, New York. I was raised and brought up in the church by my two loving parents. Growing up as a child in New York City, I saw and experienced a lot of things. Even though most of my time was spent at church with my family, I was always curious about the outside world; the street life. When I became of age, I finally got a taste of what the world had to offer.

After a while, I started drifting further away from the church; until one day, without realizing it, I was all the way out there. I started hanging out with all different kinds of groups and people, doing this and doing that. Before I knew it, I was drinking and getting high regularly. At first I didn't see anything wrong with getting my drink on and having something for the head. After all, I still went to work and took care of my business. The crazy thing about me getting high was even though I knew it was wrong, I liked it! Now, you know that was nothing but the devil. Little did I know, that was his way of deceiving me and reeling me in like a lost fool.

Many years went by and I thought I had things under control. I can remember my mother used to tell me, "Fred, if you let the devil ride, he's going to want to drive." Don't let it be said too late, "Come on in the Lord's house before it's too late."

After a while, my life started to spiral way out of control. That's when the devil showed up and showed out. I started messing up on the job. I was constantly calling in sick or not showing up because I was tired from being up all night and getting high. I started lying about where I had been and what I did with most of my money. But most of all, I started neglecting my wife and children. I had developed the "I don't care" attitude. The drugs had such a stronghold on me until I really thought I was a lost cause and bound for hell. I was so far gone; at times I didn't really know who I was or what was going on. I can remember one night waking up in the hospital and not knowing how I got there. The doctor came in and said, "Your body won't be able to take these drug binges much longer."

That alone should have woken me up and brought me to my senses; but no, I continued to get high. I was at the lowest point in my life, and I didn't know what to do or who to turn to.

One day when I felt like I didn't really have anything to live for, I took a good look at myself in the mirror. I was shocked to see how badly I looked, and how much weight I had lost. I just broke down and cried out to the Lord to please help me, and He did. I heard a small voice saying,

"For lo I am with you, even until the end of the world."

I'm from a family of prayer warriors, especially Mom. They prayed the prayer of faith for my deliverance.

To make a long story short, I wound up here at Faith Farm. When I got here, I didn't know anybody or what to expect. I just left it in God's hands and He took care of the rest. My life force and health started coming back. Once I got better, I got homesick and was ready to go back home. After one of the church services, I was walking back to the dorm with my head down, contemplating whether I should stay or leave.

When I came around the corner near the laundry room, I noticed there was a cross carved in the cement on the ground. Above the cross it said "Don't Quit." As I started to walk on, I also noticed the word "Fred"! I stopped dead in my tracks and read it again. "Don't Quit—Fred." Something went through me that I can't quite explain. I developed goose bumps all up and down my arm. Deep down in my spirit, I knew it was the Lord speaking directly to me. I looked towards heaven and said, "Lord, I hear you and I receive it."

I went on forward in the program and completed it. I must be honest; it had its ups and downs. But through it all, I finished my course. I truly learned a lot about the Bible and what it really means to me. It has helped me to reshape my life and has given me a very positive outlook on the things that really matter. It is the true Word of God. John 8:36 states:

> If the son therefore shall make you free, ye shall be free indeed.

I'm here to tell you that Jesus took off the handcuffs of hell and freed me from the bondage of addiction. He also said,

> Because I live you may live also.

I no longer have to live like that. I might not be the man that I should be, but thank God I'm not the man I used to be. All the glory belongs to God. I can see clearly now; the smoke is gone!

I would like to thank God for this lighthouse such as Faith Farm. It was a weigh station for me to make things right with God and myself. I would also like to thank everyone here who has helped me to change my life. May the Lord continue to pour out His blessings on this place.

Evan

Authors Note: *Evan is a 300+lb, Brooklyn, Jewish Pro-Wrestler. The contrast of seeing this huge, hunk of a man tenderly handling a fragile 1-3 day old dairy calf, gently bathing it and bottle feeding it, was a sight to behold. In fact, Evan will say that the caring for this gentle, fragile member of the farm community, from birth to standing and feeding on its own, was primary in his recovery. He had to take his mind off of himself and focus as a caregiver on another of God's creatures. This softening happens often at the Okeechobee Faith Farm campus.*

As a Faith Farm student, I've attended 9 graduations. At the onset of each graduation ceremony, Dean Webb or Wayne Richardson would relate to these events as a "Pay Day": Evidence of hard work, enduring faith and sound mind. I want to give you an example of what my pay days were like here at Faith Farm.

Upon my arriving at the Okeechobee campus, I was given the work assignment as a calf caretaker. My thinking was muddled, because I believed I was better than that. I believed I had the skills to make a difference in other work assignments, like trucking. I had no problem if they wanted me to make pizza every day, or even an office position ... but cows?

The time had come for me to do what I said I was going to do. So, I went out to pasture. The transformation was awesome. Upon my arriving at the calf field each morning, those little baby calves would see me, and they would skip around and make funny sounds, which I perceived as sounds of joy. I've come to learn that a cow is one of the gentlest creatures; and when asked how I respond to God's Word, my heart would react as if I were a calf loosed from its stall ... being able to love, once and for all. That was my "Pay Day".

I am certain that it was God's intent to take this 50 year old Jewish kid from Brooklyn, place me in a perfect paradise and brand me a cowboy. God organized my heart to observe Bill, my supervisor, as he loved those calves. This is where I began to comprehend what God's love was like. This is where I began to experience genuine love. I quickly recognized that I needed to see someone love something before I could love it myself. Today, I am not ashamed to profess a profound love for those gentle creatures. God answered prayers on that calf field. Nature has, indeed, become a part of my relationship with God, and I'm grateful for those babies.

My name is Evan. I lived with my parents, my sister, a brother and an overcharged beagle. My dad was a World War 2 Army hero; and for years, he battled in the Philippines. As a kid, I'd often sneak in his room and search for stuff in his dresser drawers; once finding shocking war photos. At a young age, I recognized that my dad endured extreme emotional pain. It would hurt me, and I didn't know how to help him. I lived in an apartment building where the majority of my neighbors were Holocaust survivors. I found comfort visiting with them, and I heard of the graphic experiences of that time.

My Hebrew name is Yisrael Gedaliah which translates, "He who wrestles with God's angel"; and "God who is Greatness." I attended Hebrew School where I learned that, not only did Jews not believe in Jesus Christ, but that we were becoming extinct. The Jewish teachers in my life did not feel I was intelligent enough to decide who the Messiah was, so I believed what they told me. I remember once asking my teachers what God was like, and they couldn't answer me. So, I had no relationship with God. I had a Bar-Mitzvah, and my parents went to great lengths and unlimited expense for me to have traditional Jewish instruction. I did believe and understand that God made me and gave me life.

98

My mom and dad wanted me to be a happy kid. My greatest childhood memories are them simply telling me that they loved me, which was always. I know they did their best for me, but the reality was that they lived very hard lives.

I was born late in their lives. I was referred to as their love child, and that title was very cool.   But, something went wrong. I began to witness their physical and emotional pain. I experienced stuff that I just didn't understand. At the age of 13, my brother and sister had already married and moved on. My dad was disabled from the trucking business, so he gambled and hung out with his friends. My mom was always at work, and I returned from school to an empty home. I felt lonely. I was frustrated and angry. I accumulated an odd list of complaints as if the arrangement wasn't working, and chose to use the same breath God graciously gave me to curse Him.

I took to the streets playing the role of a tough street kid, while aligning myself with a species so deceived they lusted for God's job. I was assured that I would be strong by their side. Within a short time, I witnessed tragic stuff, and eventually, I went to jail.

When I got out, I excelled in school and all sports. My goal was to further my participation and become a sports professional. I was chosen to matriculate in the first vocational high school in New York.

Aside from athletics, my hobby was to read about famous living people and then write to them. They would reply to me with letters that had amazing content and financial value. Through my writings, I became friends with Maime Doud-Eisenhower, George Burns, Andy Warhol and Senator/VP Walter Mondale. In my mailbox, it was not rare to find a handwritten letter from Dr. Christian Barnard with a hand drawn diagram of his first heart transplant. William Shockley sketched his blueprint for the transistor for me. Neil Armstrong would overload me with handwritten moon-walk quotes. Judge John J. Sirica and New York Mayor, Abraham Beame, would check-in on me, while encouraging me to learn and succeed in practicing law.

These experiences enabled me to be recognized for my unique approach. I began encouraging students to embrace the hobby. I consistently requested to speak at various upscale conventions and auctions that were frequently held in New York City. I gained membership at clubs; like the Manuscript Society, Pen and Quill and the Universal Autograph Collector's Club (UACC). I had gained unrivaled education in this field; and, as a teenager, I amassed the largest collection on the east coast. Soon thereafter, I converted from collecting to dealing in presidential documents and sports memorabilia.

In the course of my journey to Manhattan, I met journalists for pro wrestling publications and was invited, as their guest, for the wrestling matches being held that evening at Madison Square Garden. Subsequently, I was invited to join the private get-together at the wrestler's hotel, where I was approached by a well-known wrestler/manager. Lou Albano asked me if I would consider becoming a wrestler. Although I was in my early teens, I understood show business. Being a big kid, I would fit the part.

Rather than speak, I just looked at him and my silence must have encouraged him to tell me how he got his chance. "Hey kid, this is how I got my shot. Just like you, I was a big guy in the right place, during a high-spot in time." On that day, Captain Louis Albano became my guiding light to the world of professional wrestling. To become licensed as a pro wrestler, all that was required was some involvement, esteem from my fellow wrestlers and references.

I quickly learned this unique trade, fashioned my appeal and gimmick. Even though I wasn't of age, fellow wrestlers vouched for me to the state athletic commissions. In those days, formal proof of identity wasn't significant. If my cause was backed by famous pro wrestlers, then that was good enough for the politicians collecting a share of the ticket sales. I was to become an attraction: A heat builder that would put people in the seats. In Baltimore, Bruno Sammartino had just dropped the championship belt to Superstar, Billy Graham, and the World Wide Wrestling Federation was grooming my character to be a cultural magnet. Here I am, a Jew to the bone, playing the role of an Italian wrestler: "Ladies and gentlemen! Now coming down the aisle, led by his manager, Captain Louis Albano; Hailing from The Isle of Malta, and weighing 320 pounds; here he is; the Italian Stomper; The Sicilian Rock; Domenic Giovanni."

I dropped out of high school trusting I had met my aim of becoming a professional athlete. I journeyed to incredible cities and was making unbelievable money. Moreover, far and wide, people believed I was special. They desired to be around me. The more attention I received, the more I began expecting. And, in due course, I craved attention.

I was exposed to the popular drugs of the 70's and was attracted to the lifestyle. By age 18, my identity was governed by drugs and a need to be valued. Several years later, the state athletic commissions learned that I falsified my initial wrestling application; that I had been untruthful about my age. I failed to reveal my juvenile justice intervention. I was suspended for two years. I was shattered.

Although I continued to use drugs, I did accomplish much. I completed school and studied the law. Many were optimistic for my future. The best was yet to come. I lingered around other sports, where I developed into a prospect. I began a small dry cleaning business and sports marketing promotion. Yet, regardless of what I accomplished that I perceived as good, I was unable to hold onto it ... As if a man would try to hold the wind in his hand!

By age 18, I habitually depended on drugs and lived an extreme lifestyle, which led me to jail. I've spent the majority of my adult life incarcerated. My only contact with religion while in prison was when a chaplain called to tell me someone died ... period!

Although I had a hope that my parents were with God, I was an atheist. On September 11, 2001, something happened. Amidst the tragedy of that day, my son, Johnny, who was 6 at the time, says to me, "God Bless the people who died. God Bless God! God Bless Jesus! God Bless everyone! And, God Bless me and you forever." Although I didn't know where this "God stuff" was coming from, I'm grateful that I chose not to point to the burning towers as an illustration; as proof that God doesn't exist. Since that day, I've slowly been transformed. I've learned that trying to prove God exists is like defending a raging bull. It *don't* need your help ... just unlock the cage!

Let me now move on about how my debt to Him has been paid. My life was a series of bottoms, and I pray I'm done. I believe my breaking point came from an understanding that the same pain I feel, others feel, too. That really sucks!

As I was awaiting another prison sentence, I met my now good friend and brother, Mark, and I was introduced to Faith Farm. Although I refused to insult the court and request going to Faith Farm as an alternative to prison, I made a commitment with Mark to stay the course and enter Faith Farm upon release. I kept that commitment. While at Faith Farm, I finally grieved the death of my parents. Much like my parents wanted only good for me, God wants so much more.

I am His Masterpiece! I believe that the four corners of Judaism are Abraham, Moses, David, and ... Jesus. Jesus not only paid the ultimate price for me, but He is the express image of the Father. Continuing the ministry of Jesus is continuing the ministry of love.

My dream today is so big that only God can fulfill it: It's remaining in relationship with Him and living a loving lifestyle; to be a father to my son; to help others and hurt no one. I need God's help and your prayers for that.

I further hope to help others that are going to where I have been, to touch hard and hurting hearts and to share the Gospel by affirming that nobody ever gave up on me. That includes everyone here. Thank you.

I take with me a life verse, which is Proverbs 11:29:

> He who troubles his own house shall inherit the wind
> and a fool shall be a servant to the wise.

I've caused trouble to myself and others, and it seemed I was to end up with nothing while aimlessly enduring incarceration. Rather, God is making all things work together...for good.

Steve

Author's Note: *God uses the circumstances of a pet Boxer combined with a previous Faith Farm graduate and a veterinarian to allow Steve the comfort and peace to enter Faith Farm.*

Good morning, church. My name is Steve. I was born on August 5, 1973, in Fort Worth, Texas. I am 40 years old. I Timothy 1:13 says,

> *I received mercy because I had acted out of ignorance and unbelief.*

For 39 years of my life, I have acted out of ignorance and unbelief, and God has been merciful to me. From age 6, I grew up in Orlando, Florida. My father, Ken, was an international business executive and my mother, Katherine, was a stay at home mom. They divorced when I was 18, and thank the Lord it was amicable. They both eventually remarried, and they stayed wonderful friends.

In 2012, my mother passed away from complications from a surgery. Thank you, Lord; I was sober and by her side. God has blessed me with a wonderful father, my step-mother, Linda, and step-sister, Robyn. I have an amazing brother named Brian, who is 3 years older, and an awesome sister-in-law, Kelly. I also have two nephews, Evan (8) and Cole (5). My family has never given up on me, and I cherish their presence in my life.

Throughout the years, my family has been tremendously stressed and our relationships strained due to my alcoholism and addiction. At the root of our family, there is still an unbreakable foundation of Love; a love that has persevered through tough and tragic events; a love for one another that has prevailed enough that I am blessed to have them here today. They are still 100% supportive of my efforts

105

to change.   At this time, will my family please stand and be recognized!

Throughout the Bible, there is scripture that commands us to Honor our Mother and Father. Dad and Linda, I Love You; I Honor You. Let the rest of my life make you proud of me. My biggest regret is that my Mom, Kathy, is not still here so I could Honor her in a way unlike I was ever able to before.

I also have a 9 year old son. He slobbers a lot, he sheds profusely and he has bad breath. His name is Bruno, and yes ... he is a dog. He is a Boxer, and he has been my ultimate companion throughout the years. In the darkest days of hell on earth in my addiction; Bruno was always there to keep me company when I was alone, devastated, broken-hearted and confused at my life.   I have a story to share with you in the latter part of my testimony about Bruno.   It is an orchestration of events that could only come from God.   It is proof that God's sovereign power can make what seems impossible, very possible. God has the power to reverse even overwhelming odds.

As a child, I always struggled with feelings of insecurity and anger. I was uncomfortable being me. I was a bit of a chubby kid, and food was my comforter for many years. My father's career was highly demanding, and his success allowed our family to want for nothing. I was a momma's boy, but both parents loved us equally.

My interests as a child and teenager were in music. I was a drum player, and I dabbled in piano. I did not have an interest in school, and I was not a good student. My insecurities as a kid manifested themselves in a variety of dysfunctional behavior. Fighting, lying, manipulating and other acts of rebellion were defining characteristics of mine. At an early age, it became all about Steve.

As far as spirituality or religion; I was baptized Catholic, but church was rarely attended. By no means did I know the Lord. Thus, as I mentioned before, I lived a life based in ignorance and unbelief.

At age 15, I discovered alcohol and high school parties. There was an immediate relief and release that I enjoyed when consuming alcohol. I graduated high school, began community college and soon discovered ecstasy, electronic dance music and the Orlando and South Florida late night club scene. I traded my drums in for some turntables and began to pursue being a club DJ. Alcoholism and drug addiction ran rampant in my life. My life was full of chaos and drama.

In 1996, I was introduced to my first detox and subsequently, Alcoholics Anonymous. For the next 17 years, I would endure a battle of sobriety and relapse. Romans 7:15 says,

> *I don't really understand myself, for I want to do what*
> *is right, but I do not do it. Instead, I do what I hate.*

The amazing aspect about my testimony is even when I wanted nothing to do with the Lord; He protected me and shielded me from great harm. When I was sober, His grace led me to many blessings. Sobriety without the Lord still afforded me good things in life. I completed college at the University of Missouri and graduated with academic honors, Magna Cum Laude.

I met and married a wonderful girl, I was blessed with a career in medical device sales, I bought a new home and the list goes on. I found my identity and self-worth in those things, and what I really found was that I was still lonely and empty. Instead of doing what would have been right and just for all the blessings I had, I did what I hate. In my adult years, alcoholism and drug addiction would send me to detox countless times, as well as numerous in-patient and outpatient treatment facilities. I have also had 2 suicide attempts. I

107

lost everything on 3 separate occasions. Unbelievably, I have never been arrested.

Never once, until Faith Farm, did I discover the Lord Jesus Christ and the Word of God. Having been given so many blessings from God in a life without recognizing Him, I am trying to imagine my life in sobriety with Him: Worshipping Him, loving Him, seeking Him and honoring Him with the way I live my life. Philippians 2:12-13:

> *Work hard to show the results of your salvation, obeying God with deep reverence and fear. For God is working in you, giving you the Desire and the Power to do what pleases Him.*

Every question I have ever had about my life has been answered by studying the Word of God. In many areas of my life I have asked, why me; and ... why not me? There is one answer to all those questions in all areas of my life. The answer is God's Grace!

God works in people and through people to accomplish his purpose. I will close with a story about Bruno, my Boxer. This story is something that ignites a furious love in me for God.

Several days before coming to Faith Farm, I was highly intoxicated and desperate for help. I knew that I needed to go away somewhere for an extended stay. I actually took Bruno to my vet to have him euthanized. In my mind, there was no other solution. I saw no possible home for him to stay in and receive the care and love that he gets from me. I did not want to put Bruno through any further instability due to my addictions. Thankfully, upon arriving at my vet's office, he refused to put him down, because Bruno was perfectly healthy.

Bruno stayed with a friend while I went to detox, and my brother placed an ad on the Coastal Boxer Rescue Foundation's website for a foster home for 10 months. I lived in Stuart, about 50 miles north of here. Within one day of the ad being posted, a couple who live in Coral Springs, about 25 minutes south of Faith Farm, responded to the ad. Their names were Mike and Linda, and they agreed to take Bruno as long as he would get along with their boxer, Peanut. My brother drove Bruno down to meet Mike and Peanut. Mike asked Brian, "Brian, may I ask where your brother is?" My brother hesitantly said, "A place called Faith Farm Ministries." Mike starred at my brother and tears began to flow down both of their faces. Mike responded to my brother, "Brian, I am a graduate of Faith Farm 25 years ago!" He comforted my brother and to this day, Mike and Linda still have Bruno! Mike and Linda have opened up their hearts and their home to me and to Bruno. Mike and Linda will you please stand!

The Lord knows how much I love Bruno, and he hand delivered two amazing Christian people, who intimately know Faith Farm and what Recovery is all about, to assist in a crucial part of my journey: The care for my companion and best friend Bruno.

God made the impossible, very possible! God reversed overwhelming odds!

Psalm 119:107,

> I have suffered much, Oh Lord. Restore my life again as you promised!

Nicole

I was raised in New Jersey in a large Jewish family. I attended Hebrew School and had my bat mitzvah at the age of 13. Like most of us here, I experienced all types of abuse, verbal and physical.

Like many Christians, I also felt the hatred and fear from others because of my Jewish faith. There were many days I would wake up only to go outside and find swastikas spray painted on my house, front lawn and car windows. That was the beginning of my anger, rage and fear.

I started associating with different crowds of people and that was when I started doing drugs to be accepted. That did not work. I just continued to go deeper into my drug use. There were many times I was doing lethal concoctions of cocaine, GHB, crystal, ecstacy and valium in the hopes that I would close my eyes and never wake up.

I always knew there was something missing in my life, but I never knew what. In my search, I just continued to get high, which led me to legal troubles and being arrested. All the while, it was slowly destroying my family. I was sinking deeper into my addiction and not caring who I harmed along the way.

A large portion of my adult life was spent in and out of jail. You would have thought that would have kept me sober, but it did not. Most times, I was high before even leaving the jail parking lot, even after being in there for a year.

As I continued to sink deeper into my addiction and drifting farther and farther away from my family, I discovered opiates. I could never have thought that tiny blue pill could have such a grip on my life. It was quickly squeezing the life out of me, and I did not care about anyone. How could I when I did not even care about myself.

In February of 2008, my father became ill. In the midst of him having a heart attack, I was too high to drive him to the hospital. I made him drive himself. Eight days later, he died. I was so far into my addiction; I barely remember his funeral or the flight back to New Jersey.

After that, things continued to spiral even more out of control, and I was arrested again on August 9, 2010, after stealing from my brother, his wife and her family. That is when I knew I was sick and tired of being sick and tired. I needed to make a serious change in my life, before I lost my family completely; or even worse, ended up dead.

I was court ordered to another program but left there after just 5 months. I came to Faith Farm on March 30, 2011. That was the best day of my life. God has used Faith Farm to save my life.

Faith Farm has taught me to soften my heart, and it allowed me to love others again; and most of all, to love myself. It has taught me to hold my head up high and be proud of who I am and where I came from.

God has filled my life with peace, joy, love, strength and forgiveness, instead of anger, fear and hatred. Most of all, He has given me back my family.

It has been difficult for me here at Faith Farm, and many times I wanted to leave.

But, it says in Isaiah 43:2;

When you go through deep difficulty, I will be with you.
When you go through rivers of difficulty, you will not

drown. When you walk through the fire of oppression, you will not be burned up. The flames will not consume you.

And, He has been with me, and He brought me through the troubled waters. I also know He will never leave me nor forsake me. Even though this chapter in my life is over, I know He isn't through with me. So, I have made the decision to stay on for another 6 months, and I am excited to start the next chapter in my life.

To my sisters … ladies don't ever look back at what was. Look forward to what is to come and always remember Proverbs 31:30,

Charm is deceptive and beauty fades, but a woman who fears the Lord shall be praised!!

Niles

Author's Note: *Niles sent his testimony to us via email.*

My road to alcohol addiction started early, at age 9, when I found the keys to my dad's liquor cabinet. I tried it all, but really fell in love with his not-so-secret stash of Budweiser.

All through high school, I played sports (baseball, basketball and football), while drunk over 90% of the time. I eventually went to the University of Houston on a full-ride, golf scholarship. I stayed around long enough to earn both a Bachelor's and Master's Degree. I was drunk so much of the time at the University that I don't remember a whole lot of my time there.

After college, I was offered a job as the Warehouse Manager for one of the largest Burger King franchisees in the country. It was there I fell in love with the trucking industry and really wanted to learn to drive 18-wheelers. The owner of the company was a retired trucker who offered me a chance to learn to drive.

After a successful 20-year career, which included a lot of drinking while I was home, everything came to a crashing halt when the doctors informed me that I would no longer be able to drive 18-wheelers due to a serious back condition called spinal stenosis. I no longer had an excuse to go on the road to sober up. To ease the pain in my back, I drank. I eventually sold all of my equipment and my company and moved from South Carolina to Las Vegas. I figured that a new town meant a new start. Well, my drinking got worse and worse. Hey, it was Las Vegas; and with all the free beer I could drink, why not?

115

One morning, after a long night of both drinking *and* poker, I fell asleep at the wheel of my car—in the parking lot of my condo complex, no less. It was then that I realized I had a problem.

I remembered being at Faith Farm for a short period in 2004, so I got on a Greyhound bus and headed to the Fort Lauderdale campus. When I walked through the gates for a second time, I knew I had to finish it this time, or I was a dead man. I had totally disconnected from God and had let alcohol become the most important thing in my life.

Nine months later, November 25, 2007, I graduated from the program. During my time in the program, I was afforded the opportunity to put my experience and talent to work. Sammie, Andrew and Brother B allowed me to revamp the dispatch system to make it more efficient and easier to use. This was the break I needed to see some small measure of success.

A second measure of success came when the Director, Richard, gave us an opportunity to form a softball team. Even with a bad back, I tried out and was named the starting pitcher. It was another success for me, and I finally felt like I was on the road back to normalcy.

I stayed on after I graduated until I had an opportunity to follow a new career path—television. This, too, was a potential trap for me. It involved a person who was actively using drugs and alcohol. When I saw this, I moved on to Allentown, Pennsylvania, and I took a job with the Allentown Rescue Mission Workforce Development Clean Team as a sales and marketing representative.

Why Allentown, you ask? I went to high school about 20 miles from there and still have many friends in the area. The people I work for now are also in the business of helping recovering addicts and alcoholics.

I am truly blessed to have gone through the pain and difficulties during my 19 months at the Farm. It gave me a great foundation to live my life. I have now been sober over 31 months, and God isn't done with me yet. I have found a great church home in Allentown; New Bethany Evangelical Christian Church. In fact, the schooling that I went through while at the Farm is being put to good use. I am the sound technician for the praise and worship team at the church every Sunday and Wednesday.

Anyone who asks me how and where I got sober, I tell them Faith Farm. I am proud to say that I am a success today because of the principles that the Farm taught me; and with God's continued mercy and grace, I will continue on this path.

Thank you.
Niles

David

Author's Note: *A recent phenomenon in the last decade has been the increase in addictions to pain medications prescribed to mitigate pain after an accident. Often, this leads to trying additional drugs which makes the problem even worse. David sold everything he had, or gave it away, to commit to entering the Faith Farm program.*

I was born on January 7, 1971, in Clifton, New Jersey. I am the oldest of two. My sister, Jennifer, and I moved to Fort Myers, Florida, with our parents in 1977. I was raised in a Christian home. In 1983, I attended a Christian school, where I accepted Jesus Christ as my Savior and friend.

My grandfather taught me good moral values and how to help others whenever I could by following the example he set for me in our community. I tried the best I could. Not building on my new relationship with God, I started to slide into a long life of sin.

I had my first beer when I was 12 years old. The older I got, the more I drank. I was very active in sports all throughout high school, and drinking was the thing to do. It was socially acceptable. Three months before my graduation in 1989, I quit school due to my drinking and marijuana usage. Later that year, I got my GED; my parents got a divorce; my mom was diagnosed with cancer due to smoking; and, I had started a lawn maintenance business with my brother-in-law. To say the least, it was a busy year for me.

In 1992, after a 3-year battle with cancer, my mom passed away at the age of 48. She is in Heaven now where there is no more pain or suffering; where I will see her again. This is where my life started a downward spiral emotionally and spiritually. I was angry at God and my mom. I gave up my business, I didn't work for the next 2 years and I spent the small fortune my mom had left me. All I did was party and gamble.

In 1993, I got married to my high school sweetheart. That same year, I bought into a small Italian pizzeria in my neighborhood. After a short time of sobriety, I began to party and gamble again. I sold my share of the business.

On October 19, 1999, my son Joshua was born. This was one of the happiest days of my life to date. God had blessed me once again. Soon after, we purchased a house and some investment properties. Life was good, so I thought.

In 2002, I started Hopwood Enterprises; a landscape, irrigation and sod company. With the new construction boom, we were doing over a million dollars in sales and had a workforce of over 25 employees. I still continued in my sinful ways. I had everything I needed in life, except a relationship with God. I began using painkillers for my shoulder and back pain that resulted from one of 6 major accidents I had been in over the years. All the accident vehicles were totaled.

What started out to be a helpful thing for me, the devil quickly turned into an evil thing. Once I realized that taking these pills would make me forget all my pain and misery from the sins of my past, it was on.

I tried cocaine for the first time in my life at the age of 35. I wanted to make up for lost time, and I was off to the races. On a road to destruction, minutes turned into years. Before I knew it, I was divorced and had lost another business. Not only did I lose it all, I felt like I was dead. (I gave it away; it was a choice I had made.) Really, I had wished I was dead. Satan had me right where he wanted me.

Even though I had my friends, family and God on my side, I felt alone, afraid and horrified about where my life was going. I was knocking on death's door.

Broken physically, emotionally and spiritually, I cried out to God. Once again, He heard me. He told me to call Southwest Florida Addiction Services. For the third time in my life, I was in this detox center. This time God had a plan for me; I just didn't know what it was. My sister had heard about Faith Farm from a friend, but I didn't know much about it. All I knew was that it was a Christian-based program. I knew that I needed to get my heart right with God and start building the relationship with Him that I had been putting off for the last 30 years.

Not knowing what the heck I was doing, I left my house to a roommate I had only known for 5 months. I gave away most of my clothes to Teen Challenge, and I sold my Jeep and what was left of my possessions. Then I went to my sister's house to wait to go to Faith Farm. Romans 8:28 says,

> And we know that all things work together for good to those who love God, to those who are called according to His purpose. (NLT)

Within weeks after I left my house, it was broken into. My roommate was pistol-whipped, beaten to a pulp, and taken to the hospital. After he was released from the hospital, he was arrested due to selling oxycodone, dilaudid, and heroin to an undercover informant. My house had been under surveillance due to drug activity for several months. After a short time in jail, he bonded out and was killed that night. If I hadn't stepped out in faith and left everything, I would have been right in the middle of all that mess. Thank you, Jesus, for your grace and mercy.

That's how I ended up on those green benches waiting for intake. As soon as I crossed over the bridge to Faith Farm property (In God's Time), I felt the Holy Spirit. My dad even mentioned His presence. I knew I was in the right place.

The first 3 months at Faith Farm were rough. I knew where I was, well not really. I was in a daze. As time progressed, I listened in class, prayed a lot and read the Word.

One verse given to me that helped a lot was Isaiah 26:3,

> You will keep him in perfect peace, whose mind is stayed on You, because he trusts in You. *(NLT)*

For the first time in a long while, I finally started getting some clarity, even though I had to deal with phrases like "Faith Farm Son"; "It will be alright"; and "Pray about it."

I knew I was destined by God to be here. In Class 3, God revealed to me that by obeying the authority that was placed above me, I was obeying God. That's all I needed to know. Being my own boss for so many years before this; I had a problem with authority. Romans 13:1-2 says,

> Let every soul be subject to the governing authorities. For there is no authority except from God, and the authorities that exist are appointed by God. Therefore, whoever resists the authority resists the ordinance of God, and those who resist will bring judgment on themselves. *(NLT)*

In Class 4, God revealed to me that I needed to forgive my mom for dying on me. I did what He commanded me to do. By doing so, I can now speak about her and her death. It only took me 20 years; (In God's time!)

During Class 5, God revealed to me how to become Holy like Him. I Peter 1:15-16 says,

But now you must be holy in everything you do, just as God who chose you is holy. For the Scriptures say, you must be holy because I am holy. (NLT)

In everything I do, I will lean on God.

Class 6 has been an awesome experience for me. God revealed to me how to look past everything that is going on in my life and stay focused on Him. He let me use this gift right away.

One long day, there was trouble brewing in the store, and I was right in the middle of it. Before I knew it, I was on the lawn crew and then kicked out of the program … let back in and put on the house crew until further notice; all within an hour. I felt like I was in a tornado. I prayed that night for God to take this situation and all the pain, anger and resentment that was building up inside of me. For the first time in my life, I felt God take it from me. It was gone … just as fast as it built up, God took it away.

I woke up the next morning full of joy, peace and gratefulness, even without knowing what was going to happen next. I talked with James and explained the situation to him. God spoke through James, and shortly after, I was allowed back into the store at my post in outside sales. I tell you this because, (a) God told me to, and (b) it will help someone else.

If you are following God's will in your life, you will be tested. The devil doesn't like what you are doing. He will use anyone he can to get you away from God's calling for your life. He doesn't want you to find your calling. He fears that because he knows God is going to use us for His kingdom and glory.

123

I leave you with this: If you believe that God is in control, and you are doing His will, everything else will fall into place. *Everything!*

I must go now and start my ministry at home with my son, which has been confirmed by God through two different people. I want to thank God for bringing me to this holy place, and for everyone who makes this place work the way it does.

Levi

Hi, my name is Levi. I am 31 years old and I'm from Clearwater, Florida. I came here mentally, physically, and financially broken. I came with a promise to myself and my mom; that I would leave here mentally, physically and spiritually stronger. God blessed me with every opportunity to do so.

I believe I was led here to Faith Farm by God through a prayer I sent out a couple of weeks prior to winding up in Pinellas County Jail. I asked God to please get me away from this chokehold that my addiction was causing on my life, because I was running out of options. By this time, I had been contemplating ending my life.

God answered my prayer while I was in jail. I was still in medical for my withdrawal from opiates. A young man sat up as I was walking back to my bed—a young man I had never met before. He asked me if I believed in God. I answered, "Yes!" He then told me to take down the information to Faith Farm Ministries.

It was not until around Class 2 when I began to learn who God is, what Jesus stood for, and the amazing power of the Trinity as a whole. On February 17, I was baptized; finally becoming dead to sin and alive to my Lord and Savior Jesus Christ. The following week, I received my results from the local health department and found out I tested positive for hepatitis B. The nurse told me I was still infected from 2008, and since I was never treated, it's now considered chronic.

Just a couple of weeks prior, we had a guest speaker named Santos give his testimony, and I remembered him mentioning that he was healed of his hepatitis without treatment by putting his faith in God. Therefore, once I found out I still had hepatitis for the second time; (apparently so blinded by my pill addiction I had forgotten all

125

together about being positive in 2008), I began praying for help and standing in Church, whenever prayer for healing was offered.

I was told I should begin treatment as soon as possible. On March 1st, I went to the medical center in town to give blood in order to begin treatment. The following week, I returned for my results. While in the waiting room, I began reading my Psalms for the day and highlighting parts of the Scripture I really enjoyed. As I completed highlighting a piece of the Scripture, two women sitting across from me asked if I minded reading it out loud. (Only in Okeechobee, I thought!) I began reading Psalm 40:1-3:

> *I waited patiently for the Lord to help me, and He turned to me and heard my cry. He lifted me out of the pit of despair, out of the mud and the mire. He set my feet on solid ground and steadied me as I walked along. He has given me a new song to sing, a hymn of praise to our God. Many will see what He has done and be amazed. They will put their trust in the Lord.*
> *(NLT)*

Shortly after, I was called into the doctor's office expecting the worst. Reading my results, the doctor began to look at me. Puzzled, she said she wished half the people that came into her office had results as healthy as mine. She said I was not going to need any treatment. There was no sign of hepatitis B in my blood work anymore.

That day, I learned just how awesome God is. I am truly thankful that my prayer was answered. God showed me just how powerful His healing and redemptive hands are. I came here teetering on foreclosure of my home, in debt, and an addict. Also, I was in fear that I had blown any chance of ever owning and operating my dad's air conditioning company.

126

I stand here before you proud to have Jesus in the driver's seat of my life. I am mentally, physically, and spiritually stronger. My home was saved and sold with a profit. My debts have been paid, and the doors to a promising future have been reopened. I am truly thankful for the redemptive power of our Lord and savior, Jesus Christ, and anticipate living my life through His guidance and will.

I'd like to thank the staff for inviting me into their Faith Farm home, making me feel welcomed and helping me begin a new life in Christ. Thank you all!

I'd like to leave with my life verse, which is Mathew 6:33:

> Seek the Kingdom of God above all else and live righteously, and He will give you everything you need.
> (NLT)

Jeffrey

Author's Note: *Jeffrey came back to Faith Farm a second time. At least he admitted to himself that he needed more time and more Spiritual input in his life and returned. That takes courage, as well as knowing yourself.*

I was born October 3, 1988, in Somerville, New Jersey. I was raised by my dad and moved from New Jersey to Pennsylvania. The atmosphere around me was usually filled with drugs and alcohol. But truly, by the time I was 9 or 10, I was used to it. I felt like it was the normal thing to do. Around the age of 12, I tried my first joint. After that, I would try to find ways to do it again. I thought it was cool. Everybody did it.

I turned away from all my friends that made good grades and took life seriously—my real friends. I was turning into a different person and after my dad and I got into a fight, I started failing in school, and I didn't care.

This is where I fell into a very depressed state of mind. It wasn't until my mom and her boyfriend at the time, came and got me to live in North Carolina, that I lived without using and drinking.

On April 18, 2004, I lost my dad due to long-term drug and alcohol use. This bothered me, but deep down, I forgot who my dad really was. There were times he was very abusive, like when I didn't perform in school or sports. On the other hand, he taught me good life lessons, like how to be polite and to do my best in everything I do.

I have to say that being the man I am now; it affects me not to have a dad. I think this is why Jesus makes Himself known to me so much. The only real time I experienced God in my life is when I was younger. During the summer, I would go to the Catholic Church once

129

a week. This was a part of my life when the seed was planted. During my sophomore year of high school, while living with my grandparents, I received Holy Communion and Confirmation. But after I left their house to move back to North Carolina, the tables turned. I walked away from the church and did my own thing. I lost my girlfriend of a year that I truly loved, and I fell down hill quickly.

I was hanging out with the wrong people, drinking heavily, smoking marijuana and cigarettes. It got worse and worse; drinking until I didn't remember anything from the night before. There was a time when I came close to death, waking up to gargling vomit on my friend's floor. This was a time in my life where I needed God in my life; and boy, did He show up!

I went to live with a couple I knew for 30 days so I could straighten up and get God in my life. During that time, I attended church twice a week and listened to a lot of Baptist preaching. I also had one of the best experiences of my life, when Brother Chuck was talking about getting saved and what it meant. Due to the blood that was shed on Calvary's tree, on November 12, 2010, at 8:30 AM, I accepted the free gift of eternal salvation.

Since that day, I've truly never been the same. After I left their house, I moved to Florida. I lived in a couple of halfway houses until I had nowhere to go because of my drinking. I called Faith Farm, talked to Brother John, and had my first "top bunk experience." I made it all the way to Class 6, but because the lack of confession and my past sins still haunted me, I went out and medicated and was dismissed. This was one of many bad decisions I made. Here I was again with nowhere to go. You'd think by now I would have learned my lesson.

After going around the circle again; going back and forth between staying sober and drinking, I returned to Faith Farm for the second time on July 3, 2012.

The first week I was here, I cried out to God, "No more, I'm tired of going back and forth." I was completely delivered from cigarettes and alcohol.

In Ephesians 5:8-9 it says,

> For you were once in darkness, but now you are the light in the Lord; walk as children of light, for the fruit of the Spirit is in all goodness, righteousness and truth. (NIV)

One of the things that helped me at Faith Farm was confessing my sins to someone I trusted; putting everything out there, forgiving myself and others that hindered and bothered my soul. I have been giving the devil too much credit. I'm my own worst enemy; that's why putting the flesh to death is very important.

Romans 13:14 says,

> For I know that in me, that is in my flesh, nothing good dwells, for will is present with me, but how to perform what is good I do not find. (NIV)

I have to know and keep in mind at all times, no matter what I do in my life, Christ has to be the center of my attention. Without Him, I am nothing.

Faith Farm has given me a chance to have a relationship with Jesus Christ, to get my mind right and to figure out what's really important in life: God, people and spreading the gospel. For my brothers and sisters,

131

Galatians 6:9 says,

> *Let us not grow weary in doing good, for in due season*
> *we shall reap if we do not lose heart.* (NIV)

When you feel like you can't go on anymore, just remember what Christ went through because of His love for you. Trust Him. Know Him. Feel Him. There is no drug or drink in this world that is better than His love. Just give Him a chance, and He will blow your mind. After all, He created you.

Joshua

What brought me here to Faith Farm is the same thing that brought most of you. My life had, somehow, through one or more addictions to substances or compulsive behaviors, become completely and irreversibly screwed up. By the age of 28, I had become addicted to pain pills. I had done everything in my life with an all-or-nothing or a "0-to-90" attitude. That method of living didn't work out with prescription drugs.

For the last 10 years, I have been on a rollercoaster from hell; in and out of detox, halfway houses, 28-day, 42-day or month-long rehabs, homeless shelters, hospitals and jails. I had been prescribed drugs in order to keep me off of other prescription drugs.

My life had become completely and deeply rooted in all things involving chemical dependence. I had completely submerged in active use of white-knuckle assets. As you can imagine, this way of life quickly becomes unacceptable to acquaintances, friends, family and law enforcement. I had forsaken those who loved me and chosen to align myself with those who hate me and wanted to destroy me.

I had become many things that God did not create me to be; a loner, an uncaring, selfish user of people and a scandalous, deceitful liar. Those are not the words I would have used at the time to describe me, but I was more than willing to let the devil use those words to describe me. I had submitted myself and my life to the enemy to do whatever he pleased, which was nothing good.

My lifestyle had severely and completely damaged some relationships and destroyed others. You would think after all this; one would finally reach a point of desperation: the point at which you would bend your knees, extend your arms and beg God for anything that would stop this chaos. That's what I did. God answered.

I was led to Faith Farm. I called and showed up, willing to do anything it took. After being here for about 24 hours and after a night of restless detox sleep, I was no longer sure I was still willing to do anything it took. I took one look around the first morning at chapel. In my expert opinion, I came to the conclusion that everybody here is nuts.

Despite all the moronic things I've been doing the last 10 years, I still considered myself quite sane and wanted nothing to with this happiness and love. What I called it at that time was mass hysteria.

I learned that God has the ability to open doors that no one can close and close doors that no one could open. In other words, God slams shut the doors that lead to any means of escape from here. I'm stuck! God knows what He's doing. I slowly began to learn to accept there is another way, another path I could take that didn't lead to absolute destruction; a path that is the way, the truth, and the life ... Jesus!

Up to this point, I always believed in God, but I did not think God believed in me. I know now that no one could love creation any more than the Creator. I learned that the One who formed the world and created all things in it, loves me. I wanted to know that my God; all-seeing and all-knowing; could do all things, if I would just let Him. I wanted to believe.

Hebrews 11:6;

> And without faith, it is impossible to please Him, for he
> who comes to God must believe that He is and that He
> is a rewarder of those who seek Him.

134

I am on the right path at last. I am no longer those things I said I was in the past. In Philippians 3:12-14, Paul writes,

> Not that I have already obtained it or have already become perfect, but I press on so that I may lay hold of that for which also I was laid hold of by Christ Jesus. Brethren, I do not regard myself as having laid hold of it yet; but one thing I do: forgetting what lies behind and reaching forward to what lies ahead, I press on toward the goal for the prize of the upward call of God in Christ Jesus.

Graduation from the basic program is only the beginning.

I would like to recognize my family. For years, we have been fighting addiction and you always tried to keep my head above water. You never let go of the hope you had in me, and you were never willing to stand back and let your son kill himself. You have saved my life more times than I remember. I believe each of those times, you were sent by God. He was not willing to allow me to kill myself either. Thanks to all. We are all here to learn a new way of life.

Adrienne

I would like to start by thanking "Pappy" Eastham for the vision he had to help others by starting the ministry - and carrying out the will of God for his life. Also, thanks to everyone who is a part of the ministry here at Faith Farm. So many lives have been changed and come to faith in Christ because of your faithful service.

I pray my testimony touches the hearts and lives of others. Prayerfully, after hearing this testimony of what the Lord has done in my life, I hope some of you will surrender your life to Christ. Jeremiah 29:11 says,

> For I know the plans I have for you, declares the Lord:
> Plans for good and not for evil, to give you hope and a
> future.

Something very important I have learned during my journey of building a relationship with God is that God's plan has never changed for my life. It is my decision whether or not I choose to obey and follow the path God has destined for me. Because God is such a "gentle-man" and does not force us, He allows us free will. Like me, you may have chosen the wrong path long ago, ignoring the road signs of death and destruction along the way. Since God is a forgiving, loving and merciful gentleman, should I fall short and react wrongly, I can still choose to follow Him the rest of the way. In His mercy, He will bless and honor my choice. It is never too late to follow God's lead in a crisis. I Samuel 17:47 says;

> For the battle is the Lord's.

God's plan never changes. We can always choose that narrow path of His will for our life. The way that seems the easier, softer way is not necessarily the right way. My dad always said, "We are smart if we learn from our own mistakes. But, we are really smart if we learn from other people's mistakes."

I came to Faith Farm out of desperation. I was in recovery for almost 2 years when I relapsed, gave up and then overdosed. From there, I went to a detox center in Tallahassee, Florida. I was tired and lost in the wilderness when I decided to call my uncle, who is a graduate of the program and now works at Faith Farm's Okeechobee campus. I put off entering the women's ministry at Faith Farm and ended up in jail with 3 drug charges.

I believe God rescued me, yet another time, from my self-destructive behavior and my fruitless life. From jail, I called my uncle and told him I needed help. I told him I would do anything, if he would get me out. He and my aunt came, but only on one condition: that I go to Faith Farm.

I decided I was now running out of options and in a lot of trouble. I now know God will do what He has to do in order to get our attention. We can resist and just make it harder on ourselves.

Proverbs 16:1 says,

> We can make our own plans, but the Lord gives us the right answer.

God gave me four beautiful children: two girls and two boys. The past 6 years, I have been a part-time mother and a part-time child of God. He has always wanted me to have a full and complete relationship with Him, so that I can teach my children to have a relationship with Him. The time I have spent here has equipped me for this and any other "calling" the Father has on my life.

Honestly, the past 9 months have been the hardest of my entire life, but also some the best times of my life. It has been a spiritual battle within myself and against all my fleshly desires.

Ephesians 6:12 says,

> ... for we are not fighting against flesh and blood enemies, but against evil rulers and authorities of the dark world and against evil spirits in the heavenly places.

Completing this program is definitely a miracle of God! I could not have done this in my own strength. Philippians 3:13 says,

> I am still not all I should be, but I bring all my energies on this one thing: forgetting the past and looking forward to what lies ahead.

I daily surrender my life and humble myself before God and His will for my life. James 4:7 says,

> So humble yourself before God resist the devil and he will flee from you.

I have a long way to go. Several obstacles and temptations lie ahead for this next season in my life. Now I stand firm on the Word of God and hold tightly to His almighty hand.

I Corinthians 10:13 says,

> Remember the temptations that come into your life are no different from what others experience and God is faithful. He will keep temptation from becoming so strong you cannot stand up against it. When you are tempted He will show you a way out so you will not give into it.

I now listen for that still small voice and seek Him for direction so that I can stay on the path of peace.

2 Corinthians 12:9 says,

> *My grace is all you need. My power works best in weakness.*

In short, if I choose to do what I can do, God will help me do what I cannot do.

Thank you, God for loving me enough to bring me here to this ministry and for forgiving me. I am leaving with this wonderful relationship with God, and I depend on Him to carry me on His strength, not my own; because, when I am weak, He is strong.

Thank you to my family, all my sisters, the staff, Pastor and Sister Debbie for all you do to serve God. It certainly shows... I will close with this scripture:

2 Chronicles 16:9:

> *For the eyes of the Lord run to and fro throughout the whole earth to show Him self strong on behalf of those whose heart is loyal to Him.*

LOOK WHAT THE LORD HAS DONE! ISN'T GOD GOOD?

Roy

Author's Note: *On a Sunday night in November 2009, I was returning home from seeing my family in Atlanta for Thanksgiving. I turned on the TV while I was unloading luggage from the car. After my last trip in from the car, I looked at the TV screen, tuned to CNN. I noticed that they were presenting the CNN "Hero of the Year" awards from Hollywood. That broadcast was seen by millions of people worldwide. I was startled and surprised to see Roy Foster at the podium telling about his organization, "StandDown House," which helps veterans.*

You see, Roy had come through Faith Farm about 20 years or so earlier and he had made a radical change in his life. He not only found God and dropped his addictions to drugs and alcohol, but he had gone two miles north of our Palm Beach County campus in Boynton Beach, Florida, and started an outreach to help veterans. Here was a man that had been suspended from class in school as a young boy for refusing to stand and read out loud in his class out of fear, to now standing on the Hollywood stage in front of bright lights and cameras, telling his story to a worldwide audience of millions of people. He was one of the top-ten finalists out of 990 nominations worldwide for those ministries and non-profit organizations that are making the most change in people's lives.

One of the most gratifying things for me as Executive Director of Faith Farm is to see those who go beyond their recovery here, and then spend their lives helping others. And, as a retired Navy commander, I am especially gratified to those who help veterans, like Roy. Roy did that, and this is his story.

On a Friday evening in September 1990 or 1991, I was in a motel room getting high when police officers knocked at the door. They were responding to a disturbance call, and they were given my room number. There were 2 police officers: one was an older, seasoned officer; the other was a younger, eager officer. The older officer stood in the doorway preventing the younger officer from getting into the motel room. Each time the young officer maneuvered or attempted to enter; the older officer would pivot and block his access. They never gained entry. The older officer said, "I don't know if you are involved in any of this, but I know one thing, you need to get out of here." If the younger officer had gained entry that evening, I would have been in jail instead of at Faith Farm. I did have drugs and paraphernalia in the room.

I had previously been in the VA Medical Center's 30-day program. It resulted in very little change. In 30 days, I was drunk and dysfunctional again. While at the VA, I obtained a pamphlet about Faith Farm. Lo and behold, I needed another program; went looking for that pamphlet and came to Faith Farm that year. That's when I began to re-establish my relationship with God.

I grew up in the church with my parents and grandparents. Church and Sunday school was a part of my southern heritage. I knew about God, but the personal relationship with Him didn't matter to me at that time. When I came to Faith Farm, I had a feeling of peace and became engulfed in learning. What is this God all about?

As a veteran, I was very organized, thorough and methodical about accomplishing tasks. The structure at Faith Farm was not unfamiliar to me. I started as a truck driver and became the best. The first 4 months were basic service and work therapy. The body was in need of regeneration. Then, I began the Alpha Program.

The Alpha Program opened my eyes to how God really works. It reminded me of my military service: its 6-week duration; how it was regimented; the organization; structure and timelines. It brought me an understanding of the absence of God in my life.

The worship at Faith Farm was so much a part of experiencing the presence of the Lord. The fellowship with men who were seeking in the same direction is something I couldn't get anywhere else.

Pastor Mike was the pastor at that time. For some reason, he took me under his wing. Every time he saw me, we would pray. Then he would say, "Roy, God is going to do something *big* with you."

I'm thinking, "Why doesn't this man leave me alone?" But, he kept reinforcing the same theme… "Roy, God is going to do something *big* with you."

Upon completing the program, I became part of the extended, graduate program. I continued to drive the truck each day, and I had the opportunity to continue my studies, while mentoring a lot of young men that were new in the program.

During my addiction, I had lost my family. But, as I continued moving forward, God began to open doors and communication began. God starts to talk to me about reconciling my marriage. I went to California and reconciled with my wife and child. Within a year's time, I had relapsed into my addiction and found myself homeless again in California. This is what brought me back to Florida and to Faith Farm the second time.

It was Labor Day, Monday. Faith Farm was closed. I didn't have an appointment. I didn't have anywhere else to go. I was in a position to be arrested, but it didn't happen. I was totally exhausted and couldn't walk another step. I was accepted back in the program that day, when all of the rules, policies and procedures said, "No! Come back on Tuesday!" But, the door was opened and that could only be the power of God. There is no other explanation.

I had to do something different than what I had done before. Initially, I drove the delivery truck, but was promoted to be the new houseman, with a half day of work and a half day in Alpha Class. It gave me purpose: To be with 12 men; be a big brother to them; and to sit in classes with them.

Alpha taught me that God's grace is sufficient for me. That was an eye opener. Every day I listened while being taught about: God's grace and mercy; the old man and the new man; the natural man and the sinful man; Romans 6, 7 & 8; and I came to understand how it all worked together. I became filled. Hearing the Word of God *(the meat),* feeding on the Word of God and basking in His glory became a part of my very being. I finally understood that God didn't hate me and that He *does* love me. Even in my sin, He still loves me.

There was another person who played a very important role in my life. His name was George Martin. He was from Okeechobee. He wore a Stetson hat, cowboy boots and denim jeans, and he drove a tractor trailer. He was very anti-social and didn't deal with too many people. But, the one thing he did every time he came around was stop by my room, stick his head in my door and quote Isaiah 40:31 ...

> *But they who wait upon the Lord shall renew their strength; they shall mount up with wings as eagles; they shall run and not be weary; and they shall walk, and not faint.*

He quoted that to me at least once a week for the next 6 months. I didn't have a clue what it was all about, but I knew it was significant. Wait on the Lord and He will. And, He did. God opened doors and made my decisions while I simply surrendered all.

When it was time to leave Faith Farm this time, I didn't rush. In fact, it was staff that told me it was time to go. I went into a new community program called Abiding Hearts, and I began to implement some of the things I had learned to live out the truth. For the next year, God continued to groom me for His purpose. I had no knowledge of substance abuse treatments or clinical education. I wasn't familiar with AA and things that were critical for my recovery. So this gave me an opportunity to continue learning for another year.

The owner of Abiding Hearts informed me of a job opening where he worked at the Sheriff's Drug Farm. He indicated that it would be a great position for me. God was moving me into places where I had absolutely no confidence.

I am not a public speaker. I detest standing up. I was very insecure in these particular things. I had 12 guys in Alpha and moved to Abiding Hearts with 20 guys. Now, I am being transitioned into a place with 62 men, holding two 2-hour group meetings per day. For the next 8 years, I learned whatever was needed to move forward.

I was with other veterans, some who were definitely not treated fairly. I observed how some men would speak around veterans saying things like, "We don't want any crazies in here with PTSD (Post Traumatic Stress Disorder)." It was simply a hostile environment for the veteran. I decided this is not what is going to happen, and I formed a corporation called Faith, Hope, Love, Charity. It was a mission of love as described in I Corinthians 13. The fire that God planted at Faith Farm was still going; still burning, still raging.

On September 11, 2001, I was standing at the jail in the control tower with the deputies when the Twin Towers and the Pentagon were hit, and Flight 93 was downed in Pennsylvania. At that point, I decided I would resign from my job at the jail; and on December 31, 2001, Faith, Hope, Love, Charity opened StandDown House for Veterans. I knew that war was coming and that men and women were going to war. Knowing the residual from Vietnam, I had to do something. I understood exactly what was coming down the pike.

Over the next 10 years, God has been blessing the ministry. Within 6 months of opening the facility, we were adding beds and then again, more beds 6 months later. And the blessings continued.

In November 2009, I found myself standing in front of an audience of more than 70 million people at the internationally televised event, The 2009 CNN "Hero of the Year" Awards. I was selected as one of ten 10 in a list of hundreds of nominations as a CNN Hero—this God-empowered individual, who would not speak in front of people. (When I was in school, I was removed from the class and suspended because I refused to stand and read out loud.) The person on stage at the CNN Awards was not me; it was Him. I am only the vessel who surrendered and allowed God to use me. I continue to allow Him to use me without question or doubt; trusting that God is in control, and I am not; because I'll screw it up.

God continues to use me to bring about change and move things according to His plan. It is God supplying needs and opening doors, without negotiation or manipulation. God has always told me, "Wait on me!" Isaiah 40:31 states that if you wait, He'll empower you quick. I've made mistakes and have suffered consequences. But, when I'm off center, I've got to get back to that valuable lesson learned at Faith Farm.

Today, StandDown House has 36 beds, which is enough for our homeless and disabled veterans. God has showed us a new need, so we expanded our services to include homeless families. We place them into their own apartment, instead of a shelter environment. Over the last year, we've placed almost 250 families into apartments. We provide their first and last month's rent and utility start up costs. If they need additional assistance for a couple of months, we are able to help. In that same time frame, we have prevented over 200 families from being evicted through our intervention with landlords and utility companies. These are all veteran families. These are the ones that God placed on my heart and gave me to help.

Federal dollars are provided for Palm Beach County. However, veterans come from all over. We have given away a debt-free home in Margate, Florida, to a Navy veteran … a quadriplegic. God has presented 2 more donated homes in Jacksonville, Florida, and we await the cleared titles from the banks so that 2 more veterans will have homes.

We've assisted families outside of the United States as well. Daily emails are received from outside of the country asking for help. We can't help them all, but those who God places into the opportunity will receive the fruit.

The program we have now is full service. We drive to the VA early in the mornings for mental health, substance abuse and physical medical treatment. Each night, we provide a service. For example, our psychologist will provide psycho-education, or a resident may meet with their case manager about meeting individual needs. We have our Bible study groups, church every week and critical outside interaction.

We teach occupational therapy and life skills, from managing personal needs to cooking, cleaning, budgeting and shopping. The initial program is 120 days with a second phase lasting up to 2 years. Under the care of their psychologist, they learn to interact in the community and to have a safe place to come home to. The program helps them find self-worth in God. We learn to experience calmness, even when the situation itself hasn't changed. The peace that surpasses all understanding is very real.

Faith Farm has given so much to me. When our doors opened at StandDown House, everything we needed came from Faith Farm. They said, "Whatever you need, come get it." They provided all the beds, furniture, even the freezer and other kitchen equipment. This is how Faith Farm has continued to be a part of my life, even 2 years later when we were in need again. I personally need to return to Faith Farm from time to time and step foot on the grounds. It still represents a safe place, and it still has a place in my heart that is so connected to all that He has allowed me to do. As I tell the guys at StandDown, StandDown has never kept anyone clean and sober, but StandDown will afford you the opportunity. Faith Farm afforded me the opportunity.

I truly know God, and I know that I have had nothing to do with this story. I have simply been available to Him. That's it.

Damon

My name is Damon. I was born the youngest of 12 and brought up in a very dysfunctional family. My father was an alcoholic and my mother was co-dependent. To say the least, I never knew where I fit in. I was always trying to be someone I wasn't. I was an overweight half-breed, and didn't like the color of my eyes. I was always in trouble. Looking back, I was just trying to fit in.

I remember when I was 13, my half-brother molested me. And for a guy who just wanted to fit in and be loved, I allowed it to happen. I never told anyone, and for years I hated myself. I started smoking pot and hanging out with the older crowd; again just trying to fit in. It felt good and I was accepted for just who I was. At 28, I was sentenced to 3 to 5 years in prison.

I thought my world had ended, and then I heard a small voice inside me saying, "Seek Me." I did and all was well.

I got released and went back to my old ways again. I found myself drinking and drugging more than ever. I would try to seek help, but never listened to what they told me. I would always tell myself it's not that bad. By this time, I had been in and out of detox, jails and institutions.

At the age of 32, I met my wife, fell in love and had a baby. I finally felt that I fit in. The only problem was I still did not want to give up the booze and drugs. Thank God she did not put up with it. I realize now she was the best thing that ever happened to me. It wasn't long before she divorced me. Then my mom died of cancer and I felt all alone. Then there's more detox and jails.

At the age of 49, I am walking down the street. I see a hole and I fall in. The next day, I am walking down the same street and I see the same hole and I fall in again. Next day, I see the hole and I walk around it; what a concept.

I heard that small voice once again telling me to call detox, they'll help you. I went back and forth with the Father of the Universe, like I knew better. I was telling God, I've been there too many times and I have no money. He told me again. I called and the lady asked me, "How long would it take for you to get here?", and I started crying like a baby.

I told the staff at detox, "Either put me in jail or get me in a Christian-based long-term treatment program." They said "Faith Farm." I told God I would go and do anything He wanted me to do.

I got here August 29 of last year. I dove into the Word. I obeyed the ones God placed over me, and today, I can say that I have a deeper relationship with Jesus Christ and mankind. My daughter writes me often. My ex-wife speaks to me, and my family tells me how proud they are of me. I am working on my GED. I am able to help others without any other motives, and today, I can say I truly fit in somewhere.

II Corinthians 5:17 says,

> This means that anyone who belongs to Christ has become a new person. The old life is gone; a new life has begun! (NLT)

Thank you, Father God, for never giving up on me. Thank you, Faith Farm, for giving me a solid foundation. Thanks to all the staff, Pastor and Interns for pouring into me. Thanks to all of you for allowing me to fit in.

150

Bob

I was born in March 1960, in Brooklyn, New York. Our family moved out to Long Island when I was 7 years old. I had a great childhood growing up. We played a lot of sports. We had a lot of kids in our neighborhood. I started early on drinking and drugging, but it wasn't until I was nineteen that I started to do cocaine, which is when my life started to become unmanageable.

Over the next 10 years, all I did was work and do cocaine. It got to the point when it all caught up with me. I finally lost my job and went into my first rehab at twenty-nine. After I completed the rehab, I moved down to Florida, and actually did well for a while. It was only a matter of time before I got back on cocaine, and basically, I've spent the last twenty years or so going in and out of countless rehabs, detox centers, halfway houses and jail.

I never used at home, but I did use when I would travel around the state on business trips. It started out that I would get stuck for a couple of days, then that turned into weeks, then months. I've gotten stuck in just about every major city in Florida and even a couple of Third World countries. I was very good at cleaning myself up and getting great jobs, doing well for a while; then I would relapse, lose everything and have to start all over again.

The year before I came into Faith Farm was the toughest. I lost my mom during this period. I ended up blowing an inheritance of about $50,000 prior to me coming here on June 20 of last year. I was a mess spiritually. I had lost my soul to drugs. I realized early on that I didn't have another Faith Farm in me. What I did realize was that God was with me the whole time. It was my choice not to give my life over to Him.

When I got here, I had to humble myself and work hard. I focused on the classes and what they were teaching me. I learned that in order for me to survive, I had to trust God and surrender to His will. I learned that I had to change the way that I thought. I learned that our thoughts determine the way we feel, and our feelings determine the way we act.

Faith to me is finding answers in the heart. If you read and study any of the gospels, you know that if you do the right things, good things will happen. If you do the wrong things, bad things will happen. It's that simple. I also know that God has a purpose and plan for me to go out and help others and show them what He has done for me and what He can do for them.

In Matthew 10:10, Jesus told His disciples,

> *I am sending you out like sheep among wolves. Therefore, be as shrewd as snakes and as innocent as doves.* (NIV)

God wants us to go out and be smart without being suspicious; innocent without being naive. The challenges for you and I are great, so we have to take it seriously. We are sheep among wolves. I've been eaten alive a few times, and I have the scars to prove it. The best advice I received here at Faith Farm is to stick with my Shepherd, Jesus.

Chris

I just really want to give God all the praise for this. I don't think God lets any of us graduate without Him in our hearts. This place is too amazing at what it does for Jesus. There's just no way that you graduate without truly knowing God.

It doesn't matter how I got to Faith Farm, it's the same road most of us took. When I got here, I was broken. I was full of shame, guilt and deceit. I hated myself, I was on a few different psych meds, and I didn't believe in God. I have emotionally abused everybody in my life, whether I liked them, truly cared for them or not!

The only person I ever truly cared for was me, and what a wonderful job I did caring for myself, right? As a direct result of these behaviors, I truly believed that I had caused my mother's suicide. It was just horrible. I just indulged in a life of sin. That was before getting to Faith Farm.

For those of you who don't know, I was born and raised in Northern Virginia, right outside of Washington, DC. I come from a typical, modern-day, divorced, middle class family. Growing up, my sister and I had all of the love and support in the world. Our parents gave us anything that we wanted. We never had to work for anything and it caused a very "lackadaisical" life. I remember in high school, my friends started getting summer jobs and working after school. I decided that I didn't need to work. So, a great way to pass idle time is to experiment with drugs and alcohol.

I knew growing up that there was something missing in my life. I always knew that. But when I found the drugs, that euphoria that it originally gives you, I thought that was what I had always been missing; the party life. Probably the very first time I took drugs, I knew. I didn't know I was going to become an addict, but I knew I was going to do drugs. There was no doubt.

I got to Faith Farm about 6 months after moving to Ft. Lauderdale. When my mom committed suicide, I landed in jail. I lost everything. My dad was down here, so I moved down here, stayed at a halfway house and I did a lot of drugs there.

I ended up here because I really didn't have anywhere else to go. I remember someone saying to me, you know this is a 9-month commitment? I thought, great, I have a place to stay for 9 months. If he had told me I was going to eat chicken 3 times a day for 9 months, I don't know?

When I got here, Chris left a Bible on my bed. The first scripture I read was Revelation 21:4,

And God will wipe away every tear from their eyes; there shall be no more death, nor sorrow, nor crime. There shall be no more pain, for the former things have passed away. (NKJV)

After reading that, you know, I'm just like, *whoa*. I am here, I'm broken, I'm coming off all these psych meds and I'm full of anxiety. I didn't know anybody. Everybody's running around, "Praise God, Praise God." This scripture has stuck with me for the last 10 months, to this day.

I've learned so many things here from all of the teachers, staff and fellow brothers. It's endless knowledge. I've learned the books of the Bible. I've learned that thoughts control your feelings and feelings control your actions. It's had a huge impact on my life. I've learned to keep my thoughts centered on Jesus and the rest will work itself out. So far, that's what it's been doing. I was taught to recognize when I was building up to drink or drug, and again, to shift my focus onto God. That's certainly working.

I've learned that I was pretty angry and how to keep it in check. Ephesians 4:25-26 says,

> *Be angry, do not sin and do not let the sun go down on your wrath.* (NKJV)

Matthew 5:37 tells us,

> *Let your yes be yes, and your no be no, for whatever is more than these is from the evil one.* (NKJV)

When I got here, my "yes" meant "ask me again," and my "no" meant, "yeah, sure, OK." I had no boundaries with myself, with God or with my family. It's horrible. And for all of you going into Class 5, it will test your boundaries. I'm just letting you know.

Over periods of time here at Faith Farm, I've gone weeks, not necessarily months, but weeks, where I would just pray and pray, and I thought maybe I wasn't growing. But, I've grown as much as I've grown and always through prayer. I'd get over those moods, and I do see a little more growth in myself.

Philippians 4:6 says,

> *Be anxious for nothing, but in everything by prayer and supplication and thanksgiving, let your requests be known to God.* (NKJV)

Coming here, it wasn't so hard to start praying. Prayers, I've done it before. I've never really meant it from the heart. But, over time, with repetition, just praying; you know, I've grown closer to the Lord. I've developed a personal relationship with Him. And it's amazing.

You know, the change they say is in the heart; then, the outside comes next. But truly, I see so much change in my heart. If not for coming to Faith Farm, I can't imagine that I would even be alive. My heart really has been healing here.

I no longer blame myself for my mother's suicide. I do believe, wholeheartedly, had she not done that, I would not be where I am today. So, I don't hate her for it. I can't say that I love her for it, but I'm standing here today, and I'm graduating from Faith Farm as a true believer in God now. I'm changed on the outside and I'm changing on the inside every day.

If my Mom were still here, I would still be at home, mooching off her; spending thousands of dollars, not going anywhere, not doing anything and certainly not knowing the Lord. I don't regret any of my past anymore. It's led me here. And truly, that's what Faith Farm is all about. They take you; sick, broken. All they do is show you Christ the Healer. He does everything else. This was the hardest thing for me; to get going to reading.

You know, the whole time at Faith Farm, I would pick it up, the Old Testament; and you know, that's boring. But, once I got in the New Testament, I actually just kept reading and reading, and that's where your change in the heart comes from. That's where you have to pick up this Bible. It's hard, but once you start, it gets easier.

I just want to thank all of my brothers who laugh with me on a daily basis. This is a serious thing. This is a life or death place, period! I just want to thank all of you; Staff, Pastor, Dean Webb and especially Pappy, our founder. I just can't imagine how many lives he's saved through this ministry.... through Jesus Christ, in the last 60 years.

Henry

Author's Note: *Henry entered the program when the Fort Lauderdale campus was undergoing a massive renovation on the 50-year-old, 3-story dormitory. Adding a new sprinkler system and having to collapse the old elevator shaft to build and install a new, larger one, required that we move the students out of the dorm and into the church fellowship hall, with portable outside shower tents. During that time, not one student quit or left the program because of the disruption and hardship caused by the renovation of the dorm.*

I'm very thankful to be here today. For me this is a personal accomplishment to be able to follow something I knew was God's will for me to do. I was down in the dumps, where we've all been before, and when I heard the suggestion for me to come here to Faith Farm, I knew it was God's voice through a messenger all the way in California. That's how I'm here today standing before you guys. I had the willingness to listen, and I had the need for Jesus Christ in my life.

I avoided His presence in my life for 30 years; living of the flesh and doing what I wanted to do for a very long time. The whole time, I knew that my true higher power was Jesus Christ and the Lord, our Father. I was finally beaten down enough to where I was willing to accept that fact and do whatever it took to bring me here today.

So, I flew out from California in January. I quit smoking the day before I got here, and I've held fast on that decision. I've tried to walk upright since I've been here. I'm not perfect. I make mistakes. I offend people at times; and for that, I apologize. Other times, it's just part of my growing and part of my learning how to walk Christ-like. It's part of my learning how to accept my faults, look at them and correct them.

Through the instruction I received here at Faith Farm from staff and students, I'm able to make those adjustments and continue to do the Lord's will; remove myself from my own will and do what He wants me to do. I still have a long way to go. Education is something I want to pursue, but I'm going to put that aside until August of next year and participate as a Servant Leadership Student (SLS extended program). I feel I still have a lot to learn in the ministry and in the Word, and I feel there might be some things I might have missed through these last 10 months. So, I want to see if I can continue to receive the Word, grow in His Spirit and walk in a Godly way ... and give back.

Faith Farm has given me so much, from the clothes on my back, to the food in my stomach, to the roof over my head. It's an amazing, chaotic, wonderful place to be if you're willing to just embrace it and let go of our old ways and embrace the new. Receive all the gifts that are available to us here, because they are plentiful.

I came in during a time when they were remodeling the third story dorm, and it wasn't in the brochure when I got it. I was in hospitality for a week; then I got shifted over, by-passed from the dorm to the Fellowship Hall where it was one hundred bunks deep. We had Bass Pro shower tents in the back, and we were showering in them. For those of us who experienced that and continued to persevere through that time, it was humiliating and strengthening. It just proved that if we could go through that and survive what we came through already to get here, we can still continue to move on and forward and seek the Lord and His Light. Hats off to those who've done it, and I want to lift up those who are here.

Now, coming into the program, you're going to have challenges. You're going to have things that are going to try to pull you back to where you were. Just try to remove yourself from those situations, seek counsel and ask questions. Those around you will lift you up out of those dark times.

I've got a few Scriptures I want to read. They've helped me throughout my days here. I'm new at this. I'm forty years old, and one of the big incentives to come here was to read the Bible for the first time. I do it daily. I do it in the morning, and I do it in the evening. I need to do it more throughout the day. But, I'm practicing daily.

So, if you want to turn with me to Ephesians 6:10-16, this is about putting on the armor of God. Ephesians 6:10 says,

> *Finally my brethren, be strong in the Lord and in the power of His might. Put on the whole armor of God that you may be able to stand against the wiles of the devil. For, we do not wrestle against flesh and blood; but against principalities, against powers, against the rulers of darkness of this age, against spiritual hosts of wickedness in the heavenly places. Therefore, take of the whole armor of God that you may be able to withstand in the evil day and have done all to stand. Stand therefore, having girded your waist with truth. Having put on the breastplate of righteousness and having shod your feet with the preparation of the gospel of peace. Above all, take in the shield of faith with you that you will be able to quench all of the fiery darts of the wicked one. And take the helmet of salvation and the sword of the Spirit in the Word of God.* NKJV)

This Bible; it's got a cover, front and back; and the inside of it is an amazing story, amazing miracles and an amazing way of life, if we're open to embracing the Words in here. I've shunned away from this truth for so long. When I finally accepted it and was willing to try

159

to have it part of my daily walk, it just lessened the load of burden I had on myself.

I lost my father to his addiction of alcoholism. I had done a year of sobriety, and I had stopped communication with him, because my sponsor told me that it would weaken my walk. So, I wasn't able to communicate with him for that year. A week after I got my chip of sobriety, he took his life through suicide from alcoholism. I kind of went off the deep end, and that's what brought me here.

For 5 years, I was just running amuck. I wanted to meet him and I wanted to see him, but I didn't want to die like he did. So, now I want to live like how I know he wanted me to live, in an upright way; in a holy way. I do what I do in remembrance of him. I carry him in my Bible with me, in my heart daily and I talk with him all the time now. That was one of my last walls I had to climb over to get here today. It was to get over that and realize that he still loves me, and I still love him.

One more Scripture I want to go over is in Philippians, we've been going over this in school in the mornings and it came across to me. I wanted to share it also with you. Philippians 3:12-14 says,

> *Not that I have already obtained or already perfected, but I press on that I may lay hold of that which Christ Jesus had lay hold for me. Brethren I do not count myself as apprehended. But one thing I do, forgetting those things which are behind and reaching towards those things which are ahead. I press towards the goal and the call of that which is Jesus Christ.* (NKJV)

And that's a daily walk for me.

Last Scripture and then I'll close. This is one I've shared before. It's Psalm 25. And again, I just want to encourage all the new guys and all those who are still here at Faith Farm, but want to be where I am at today. Just continue to try and lift each other up, and study the Word as much as possible. Give what you've gotten. There's so much to share within this book.

Psalm 25, Song of David:

To You, oh Lord, I lift up my soul. Oh, my God, I trust in You. Let me not be ashamed, let not my enemies triumph over me. Indeed, let no one who waits on You be ashamed. Let those be ashamed who deal treachery without cause.

Show me Your ways, oh Lord. Teach me Your paths. Lead me in Your truths and teach me. For You are the God of my salvation.

On You, I wait all the day. Remember, oh Lord, Your tender mercies and Your loving kindness; for they are from of old. Do not remember the sins of my youth, nor my transgressions. According to Your mercies, remember me. For Your goodness sake, oh Lord.

Good and upright is the Lord. Therefore, He teaches sinners in the way. The humble He guides in justice and the humble He teaches His way. All the paths of the Lord are mercy and truth; to such that keep His covenants and testimonies for your namesake, Oh Lord. Pardon my iniquity, for it is great.

For who is the man that fears the Lord? Him shall He teach in the way He chooses. He himself shall dwell in prosperity and his descendants shall inherit the earth. The secret of the Lord is in those who fear Him, and He will show them His covenant. My ways are ever toward the Lord, for He shall pluck my feet out of the net.

Turn yourself to me and have mercy on me, for I am desolate and afflicted. The troubles of my heart have enlarged. Bring me out of my distress. Look on my affliction and my pain, and forgive me of my sins. Consider my enemies, for they are many and they hate me with cruel hatred. Keep my soul and deliver me. Let me not be ashamed, for I put my trust in You. Let integrity and uprightness preserve me. For I wait for You.

Redeem Israel, oh Lord, out of their troubles. (NKJV)

Patrick

My name is Patrick, and I am a graduate of Faith Farm Ministries in Ft. Lauderdale. Before I came to Faith Farm, all I had were the clothes on my back and a family out there somewhere who loved me and prayed. I was lost and did not love myself. I did not know God. I was living a life of darkness and sin.

As far back as I can remember, my father was an alcoholic. I grew up without him in my life, and I did not know what it was like to have a dad. My mom raised me, my two brothers and my sister as a single mother. We lived in a middle class neighborhood, and she worked hard to provide for us all.

I was introduced to alcohol and marijuana at a young age. I was 12 years old when I had my first drink and smoked my first joint. Starting from there, I began to party. It started out as a weekend thing, and then I began to use every day. My using and the influence it had on me caused me to get into fights and act out a lot in school. I made it as far as the 9th grade in high school, where I failed my first year. My 2nd year as a freshman, I was expelled for fighting. I got sent to an alternative school and dropped out of school when I was 16 years old. After that, my life involved a lot of trouble. I sold marijuana and was arrested for the first time when I was 17 years old.

I was placed on probation. I continued to drink and smoke weed, and I violated my probation because I failed to pass a drug test. At 18, my probation officer sent me to my first rehab. I did not want to be there and was in denial at the time. I could not admit to having a problem. I left the program, went back to using and failed to complete my probation. I continued to get into trouble and had been in and out of jail. I was court ordered to a few other residential treatment programs and could not control myself. It only got worse.

I could not use socially. I was not an occasional user. I had become a full-blown alcoholic. I got drunk for a living. I could not keep a job because I was either too hung over to show up, or I was in jail because I did something wrong while I was drunk.

At that time, I feel I had reached my rock bottom. I lost my place to live and became homeless. I ate out of dumpsters, went to soup kitchens to eat and bathed in canals or under water hoses. I was living a miserable life. I was depressed all the time.

In 2008, one of my best friends named Sean was a student at the Ft. Lauderdale Faith Farm campus. He found out I was homeless. He got a hold of me through another friend of mine named Serge. He would pray for me over the phone. Through him, God convinced me to surrender my life over to Him.

On April 10, 2008, I went into Faith Farm and gave my life to Christ. God has directed my heart and my life through the leaders at Faith Farm in Ft. Lauderdale. I was given opportunities and received miracles I never imagined were possible for my life. The journey was not easy. I stayed at Faith Farm for a total of 3 years and 4 months. In that time, with God's help, I became a Servant Leadership Student (SLS), I got my GED and I went to Atlantic Technical Center to learn a trade and become an electrician. I got my first driver's license.

I now have my own car and a job in my trade working as an apprentice. I am learning every day and getting the experience I need in order to achieve one of my goals of becoming a licensed journeyman electrician.

God has also blessed me with the most amazing woman in my life. We are happily married. She is my best friend and the love of my life. Together we attend church and put Jesus Christ first in our lives and marriage.

To achieve all these things, I set goals for myself and I worked very hard to accomplish each one, one by one. The most important thing was that I trusted God and had faith that he would provide those things for my life.

Since my time as a student at Faith Farm Ministries, I have celebrated my 4th year as a born again Christian. I continue to visit the farm and share my testimony as a good servant of the Lord. I am working hard every day and go to church every week.

I would like to thank God for allowing me to share my testimony of what He has done for me in my life to others. I would like to thank all the leaders at Faith Farm for giving me the tools I needed for my new path in life with the Lord, Jesus Christ.

I want to share a few Scriptures that helped me along and still continue to help me now. Mark 9:23:

> *Jesus said to him, "If you can believe, all things are possible to him who believes."* (NKJV)

2 Corinthians 5:17 says,

> *For if we are beside ourselves, it is for God; or if we are of sound mind, it is for you.* (NKJV)

Philippians 4:13:

> *I can do all things through Christ who strengthens me.* (NKJV)

And finally, Philippians 4:19:

> *And my God shall supply all your need according to His riches in glory by Christ Jesus.* (NKJV)

Anne

In her letter to Faith Farm, Anne writes:

Eleven years ago, I drove across the bridge and entered the program for women at the Boynton Beach Florida facility. I had a mixture of feelings going on inside me: anxiousness, relief, fear, depression, and sadness.

I did not know how or why, but as I drove over that bridge, I had an overwhelming sense of peace and calmness. Maybe because I had made the decision to change my ways; or maybe because deep down inside me I knew I had made the right choice to be there.

Another interesting reaction that happened is that I had a sense that I was going to be there a very long time over the required time served. I know now it was all in God's plans. Jeremiah 29:11:

> For I know the plans I have for you, declares the Lord,
> Plans to prosper you and not to harm you, plans to give
> you hope and a future.

The reason I chose Faith Farm was because it was free and I could afford that. I had just gotten two DUI charges within a month. I had to get myself in an inpatient treatment center fast; my focus was to do what was required. I did not care where, just a place I could afford and without a waiting list to get in right away before my next court date. I found Faith Farm. It was free and I would deal with the religious thing later. My focus was getting into the place.

Now remember, I was just avoiding jail and all of that business; and as I have learned about myself, thanks to Faith Farm, I am the queen of manipulation and compliance. I can conform to situations, so this religion thing: "Piece of cake" I thought; "I can handle this. I will do what they say. I will say 'yes' and 'no' and whatever they throw at me."

Needless to say, it took about 3 months of compliance, and lo and behold, the Spirit moved greatly in me. Everything that I was learning went from my head and landed miraculously into my heart. I was saved by my Lord and Savior, Jesus Christ.

I graduated from the Eastham Home for Women at Faith Farm and stayed on as a Servant Leadership Student (SLS). After serving as an SLS, I resumed my life as a professional chef and moved up to Chicago, Illinois. I was active in the church. I even hosted a Bible study/cooking demonstration class, which drew a lot of people to the study and many became active members in the church.

I was amazed I could walk along side women who had been Christians; brought up in the church. Time went on in Chicago. I found that being in the food industry was okay. However, the hours and lifestyle were not for me. I was struggling to stay in the food industry because my attitude and outlook on life had changed. I had lost the passion for being a professional chef and restaurant manager. My focus on life had changed.

I wanted to work with women who had problems with drugs and alcohol. I was ready to give back what I had received. I was diligently in prayer and meditation about what my next move in life would be. No doors were opening up in Chicago.

Then, one day I received a call from Faith Farm. They wanted me to help run the Women's Home in Boynton Beach. It was winter of 1999, and the Women's Home was going through a transition. I packed all of my furniture and other belongings, moved down to Boynton Beach and lived above the women's dorm.

As I look back now, God was preparing me for something more with each new transition I was taking on my path of life. I was so proud to be part of the staff at Faith Farm. It was an honor and a privilege to work there, and I treasure the experience I gained by working at Faith Farm. Many of my students still keep in touch with me today.

God knows! He always has the big picture in mind, and my experience working with the ladies was preparing me for what I do today. I am now a social worker at a local medical emergency room. I now help hundreds of people a year and daily take the opportunity to share what the Lord has done for me. Acts 20:24 says,

> *But my life is worth nothing to me unless I use it for finishing the work assigned me by the Lord Jesus—the work of telling others the Good News about the wonderful grace of God.*

I am pretty amazed at what my life looks like 11 years later. Today, I own my own home. I am very active in the community. I volunteer at a Christian-based food pantry. I am active in my church, Christ Fellowship, and I love my small group. I am diligent in my attendance. And, I just love all of the Bible studies.

One thing I can say is that I am proud I went through the program at Faith Farm. I am not ashamed. If by telling my story helps one person, then that's what it is all about.

The Lord took a self-absorbed, career-oriented, selfish and lost woman who just received her 5th DUI and was facing major time incarcerated; God took a woman who did not believe she had a life-controlling problem due to drugs and alcohol; and transformed her today into a beloved daughter of the Lord and Savior, Jesus Christ.

Romans 12:2 says,

> Do not conform any longer to the pattern of this world,
> but be transformed by the renewing of your mind.
> Then you will be able to test and approve what God's
> will is—his good, pleasing and perfect will.

Today, many homeless and downtrodden come daily to my window at work, and I do not hesitate to share my story with them and tell them, "Look what the Lord has done."

Holden

My name is Holden. I was born in Cocoa Beach, Florida. I was brought up in a somewhat dysfunctional family. My parents divorced when I was about 4 years old. My sister and I lived with my mother. My mother had her own alcoholic issues. It seemed to be a 24-hour party. I took my first taste of beer when I was 8 years of age. I did not like it. My mom went to rehab when I was around 10 years old, and I went to live with my aunt in Orlando. My mom came to Orlando to take care of my sister and me.

When my mom got home, I noticed I could take advantage of the situation. I'd tell my mom it was 6:00 PM when it was really 11:00 PM, and then I'd stay out smoking weed all night at friends' houses. My mom and aunt saw I was out of control, and I was reunited with my father. I moved in with him in Merritt Island. In 8th grade, I started to get in trouble. I started smoking weed and drinking a lot. This progressed into middle school, and I was introduced to percocet, xanax, 2-C-I, XTC and cocaine. I was introduced to oxycontin 80 mgs at 15 and started to smoke them regularly. I held down a job at Sears for 2 years, while going to an OJT high school program and spending every penny on oxy80s and XTC.

Between the ages of 18 and 25, I'd been to multiple detox, rehab and halfway houses. I went to rehabs costing from nothing up to $30,000, and nothing seemed to work. After leaving the programs, I got back into drugs faster and harder. I started to shoot pills and heroin, overdosing 3 times where I turned blue in the face, and my skin became pale.

My addiction became a full-time job. So, I started robbing and stealing. I stole from my dad, from my grandmother, from anyone I came in contact with, as well as people I didn't even know. Mom, Dad, Heather—I'm sorry for stealing your money and property. I'm sorry for stealing your time from you to be with me, your son and your brother, while I was in my addiction. I'm sorry for being selfish. I'm sorry for the hurt and pain I've caused you guys; when I didn't come home, and when you didn't know where I was for days and months at a time; wondering if I was still alive or not. I'm truly sorry.

The last year before I came to Faith Farm, I was at my lowest. I was spiritually broken.

Katie, my girlfriend of 5 years, and I were getting evicted out of our apartment. We moved to a friend's house. We were robbing, stealing, conning and scamming to get money for drugs. The friend's house, where we were staying, was sold due to foreclosure. Once again, we had to move. We moved into a Motel 6 for 3 months.

Then, last October, in the smoke-filled room of Motel 6, I had an epiphany. The way that Katie and I were living wasn't right. My addiction wasn't only bringing me down, it was bringing my family down and the woman I loved. I knew this wasn't the way God wanted me to live my life. I knew I had to be a man, the leader and the strong one. I had to say, "This is enough."

While Kate was out of the room, I called my dad to come get me and take me to the hospital for detox. He came, and we went to the hospital and back to the motel. This happened 4 times. The devil was trying to pull me back. I surrendered and went back to the hospital and walked in. I went to detox. Weeks later, I arrived at Faith Farm. I promised myself and God I would finish this program, and I would learn as much as I could about God, what he wants me to do and learn about myself.

I've had a lot of trials through this program where I wanted to pick up and leave. Instead, I leaned on God and not my own understanding. He has taken care of me and all that I have been worrying about.

In my past rehabs, I thought I was getting what I needed to get and stay clean. But, the one thing they weren't teaching was who God is and how much He loves us. I came to Faith Farm and noticed God is in the equation. I've held on to what I've learned in the past rehabs, and when I put God into the equation, it makes sense now. I am worthy. God has helped me change. I am a new creation in Christ. The old 'me' is dead. I am set free.

I can't stop thanking God enough. I want to thank everyone who has supported me through the program. Mom and Dad, thank you for not turning your back on me after all the horrible things I've done. You are amazing parents. Thank you.

Heather, I know we have never seen eye to eye. I do love you and thank you for all the times you drove me to detox and rehabs. I know everytime you did, you were praying, "God, I hope this is the one." Well, Heather, this is the one!

I'd like to thank everyone here. In one way or another, everyone has helped me. I also want to thank Jesus Christ. Without Him, I'd be dead. Before I go, I want to leave you with a couple of Scriptures. Proverbs 4:10-14:

> *My child, listen to me and do as I say, and you will have a long, good life. I will teach you wisdom's ways and lead you in straight paths. When you walk, you won't be held back; when you run, you won't stumble. Take hold of my instructions; don't let them go. Guard*

them, for they are the key to life. Don't do as the wicked do, and don't follow the path of evil-doers. (NIV)

2 Timothy 2:22:

Run from anything that stimulates youthful lusts. Instead, pursue righteous living, faithfulness, love and peace. Enjoy the companionship of those who call on the Lord with pure hearts. (NIV)

You're probably wondering what I'm going to do next. I'm going to stay around, work for Charlie's Landscaping and see what God has for me next.

Marrion

Good Evening, Church. My name is Marrion. I graduated August 22, 2010, and I am staying on as an extended student. Please join me in prayer: Dear heavenly Father, thank you for being with me and giving me the strength and courage to give my testimony. I pray that my testimony will inspire, encourage, help others and most importantly, bring you glory in Jesus' Name. Amen.

Like many of you, my life has been challenging and my circumstances painful. Because of this, I became very angry with God. I believed God hated me and abandoned me because He did not rescue me from my torment. My dad, the most important person in my life that I should have been able to trust, betrayed my trust in unspeakable ways. As a result, during my developmental years, I was scared emotionally. This began many years of dysfunctional living. The pain that began in childhood took a huge toll on me well into adulthood. I have learned that it is true what God's Word says in Numbers 14:18,

The Lord is slow to anger and filled with unfailing love, forgiving every kind of sin and rebellion. But He does not excuse the guilty. He lays the sins of the parents upon their children and the entire family is affected – even children in the third and fourth generations.

At this point, I did not want anything to do with God. I took control of my life and found ways to survive and numb the unimaginable pain.

My attitude towards Christ was that of his enemies in Luke 19:14,

But His people hated him and sent a delegation after
him to say, we don't want him to be our King.

I wanted to know, where was God in all of this? I have learned that He was right there beside me in my torment protecting me and keeping the abuse from being worse than it was. For this, I thank Him.

Here at Faith Farm, I have learned that God gave us free will, and that God would not stop my abusers from their bad choices any more than He has stopped me from making my bad choices that have harmed others. I have learned that I grieved God by blaming Him for the abuse that I endured and believing He allowed bad things to happen to me. It made me unhappy to see how sad I had made God by blaming Him; being angry at Him, turning my back on Him and being self-centered. I thank God that even though I turned my back on Him and hated Him, He did not treat me the way I treated Him. I know God gave me free will, and I am glad I have chosen to no longer live under Satan's control. I have chosen to quit being angry with God and stop playing the blame game. I have chosen to stop living in the past and giving the past control. I have chosen to give God control of my life. I chose to change.

The process of change was not easy or painless for me. I now know that any discomfort in honestly dealing with the root causes of my pain is far less than the recurring pain that would have continued to torment me, if I had not chosen to change. I thank God for being with me and comforting me during the changing process. I thank God that I have not allowed fear to stop me from change as it has in the past.

Before coming to Faith Farm, I had lost all hope of my life ever changing. I was afraid to trust God, but I knew deep in my heart that God was the answer. During my stay at Faith Farm, the most impactful course for me was "The Wounded Heart." This class helped me to heal, forgive myself, my abusers and most importantly, God. Having to change dorm rooms, drama class and wearing a dress helped me to learn to trust God, and together with Christ, challenge my fears with victorious outcomes.

Being placed in leadership as room lead and dispatch lead helped me to learn leadership skills, and most importantly, to overcome my fear of men. I am thankful to God for placing men in my life that helped me to see that not all men are like the men from my past. I thank the staff and my fellow sisters for restoring my trust in Christian people; for your support, teaching, listening and giving me unconditional love. This made me change my mind about Christians and even become one myself.

Thank you for allowing God to use you in your own special ways to change my life. I thank God that He gave Pappy the vision for Faith Farm; a protected space that God used to help me see who He truly is, and who I truly am in Him. Faith Farm also started me on my path to healing so I can become all that God intended for me to be. I thank God that I learned to follow the example of Christ, who was moved with compassion for sinners. He prayed for them as they nailed Him to the cross. This inspired me to forgive my dad and others who I held resentment towards for the abuse I endured.

The week after my graduation, God allowed me the opportunity to see if I had really forgiven my dad. The day I graduated, I took a vacation to Tampa. I called my only friend from North Carolina; the only person in North Carolina who would have known where I was. She broke down in tears and asked me why I called. I told her to let her know I was still alive and to start to form a friendship with her again. She told me that my mom had called her earlier that day asking if she knew where I was. She broke down in tears and told her no. Then a few hours later, I called.

I learned that my dad was in the hospital. He was not doing well and wanted to see me. This brought up many feelings for me, so I came back to the farm and we prayed. Three days later, I was on a plane to see my dad for the first time in 10 years. I thank God that my dad and I had some good conversations and are slowly starting the restoration process.

Then, in October, I went to the emergency room because I kept having pain. They diagnosed me with ovarian cancer. The doctor got mad at me because I had faith in God and was not upset. I came home and we prayed again. I went to several doctors and had several other tests, and they kept saying it was cancer. I kept praying and trusting God. I had the tumor removed, and Praise God; it was not cancerous. I could continue to thank God all day long for all the miracles He has done for me.

Last, I encourage anyone who wants to give up. Endure the long hard change process. It is well worth it. In dispatch, there is a sign with a picture of Jesus that has inspired me many times when I wanted to quit. It reads, "I never said it would be easy. I just said it would be worth it." Thank You, Church. God Bless!

Author's Note: At Faith Farm, we preach "forgiveness". We believe that one needs to truly forgive others in order to clear their hearts and spirits to receive all that God has for them. I am personally convinced that Marrion's forgiveness of her abusive father was the key factor in Marrion receiving her total healing from past offenses against her and enabled her to walk away from the hurt of past abuse by her father and others.

Michael

I was born June 6, 1957, in Manhattan, New York. I was raised in the Bronx, where I have the fondest memories. Later moving to Long Island, I had some difficulties in my adolescence concerning drugs and alcohol. I knew first-hand the negative effects and consequences that gripped many generations of my family. It was a curse. Any minor run-ins with the law were alcohol fueled.

After graduating high school, I entered the Army to escape the alcohol and drug-fueled environment. While serving in the military, I was losing more friends back home to overdoses and drug related crimes than those I was serving with in the Army.

After my enlistment, I returned to Long Island and met my wife, whom I'd be married to for over 30 years. Her encouragement and support kept me focused and on track for the better things life had to offer. Together, and with God, we raised 3 healthy children. I knew the importance of keeping my children close to the church family; having values, structure and discipline. I'm not bragging, because it's true … I was the best dad! My entire focus was my family. I was able to break the generational curse of substance abuse once and for all.

I was clean and sober for over 30 years, until that dreadful day in 2007, when I had my neck broken and was introduced to pain pills. I took them daily for 3 years, still functioning as a mental health counselor, teaching crisis intervention in 3 HCA area hospitals, running groups and tasked with supervision of clients.

I was an addict and everyone knew it. I lost my job at Columbia hospital in the Pavilion of over 20 years, my 30 years of marriage, the respect and trust of my children, my parents, brothers and sisters; and the final kicker, not being able to be with my grandchildren.

Now, being alone and far from reality, I picked up my first drink. It was a spiral down to hell. It was like dropping a brick. I was a walking dead man, prisoner within my own mind. DTs, hallucinations, delusions, you name it. I knew, during a brief moment of clarity, that God would be the only one to restore my sanity and my life. I called Faith Farm.

Intake suggested detox, then rehab. After 30 days, I began calling Faith Farm every day. Each day I phoned, he'd say call twice on this day, once on that. I was obedient, and he let me in. Since being at Faith Farm, God has restored my relationship with my family. Restoration of my mind has occurred. The Holy Spirit now resides within my soul. I have purpose and a God-given plan. I will be a testimony to the brothers just coming over "the bridge." I will give back that which was freely given to me. I will be loyal, helpful, friendly, courteous, kind, obedient, thrifty, brave, clean and reverent. His will be done! Amen.

Ashley

Dear Heavenly Father, please be with me as I give this testimony. Please help me to not be nervous or apprehensive. Let my testimony be a captivating story that ultimately gives you the glory. Let it be uplifting and inspiring to those who are struggling. Thank you for all you have done in my life. I love you and thank you for loving me, especially when I did not love myself. In Jesus' name, Amen!

The beginning of my journey at Faith Farm started in September 2011. This was, in fact, my second time here at Faith Farm. My first time coming into the program was in January, 2007, when the women's program was in Okeechobee. I left the program after about 4 months, thinking that I had it all figured out. I thought I knew what I was doing. I believed Faith Farm was NOT going to teach me anything else I did not already know. I had developed a relationship with the Lord, and I thought I was ready. So I left.

I managed to stay sober for about 5 or 6 months. Before I knew it, I was back to my old habits again, seemingly worse than ever before. It took a few years, but I finally swallowed my pride and asked to come back to Faith Farm. I was allowed to come back. That was September of 2011, and here I stand before you today.

This has not been an easy journey. I have grown emotionally. I have grown spiritually. And thanks to our wonderful chefs, I have grown physically! *(laugh)* I have had to learn responsibility, organization and how to cope and deal with every situation. I came to realize that, along with numbing the bad feelings, I numbed the good as well. So, I have had to re-learn many things.

Philippians 4:6 tells us,

Do not worry about anything, instead, pray about everything. Tell God what you need and thank him for all he has done.

I have learned to pray instead of worry. I have learned to lean on God instead of leaning on man. It has been a process in which I have had to change, and sometimes change hurts. Change makes us uncomfortable. However, with the help of the staff here and my extremely supportive family, the good Lord has gotten me through. I owe a great deal of gratitude to my mother and my grandfather who have refused to give up on me.

I am blessed to have a God who loves me infinitely. Because of Him, I was not only able to come back to Faith Farm, but I stand here as a graduate today. I owe everything I am, everything I have become and everything I ever will be to the grace of God. I WAS an alcoholic. I WAS a drug addict. With God, I am a conqueror. Now, I HAVE overcome. Thank you and Godspeed.

Dustin

I want to begin in prayer. Heavenly Father, I come to you today, giving you all of the praise and glory for what you have done in my life and for the men sitting behind me. Father God, I ask that the words of my testimony can touch at least one person in this congregation today. In Jesus' name, Amen!

First and foremost, I want to give God all the credit for my being up here today. Prior to coming to Faith Farm, I was at the lowest part of my life. I was incomplete. I was no longer in touch with reality, and I had lost the will to live an honest and clean life. I had burnt the bridges of the ones that I love; the ones that were the most important to me, over and over again. I was so wrapped up in my addiction. I didn't care about anything or anyone else; only my self-gratification.

The sickest thing is that I thought that everything was going to get better. But as we all know, it always gets worse. This is the truest definition of insanity, if there ever was one.

I was so focused on myself that I neglected the fact that my 7 year old son was watching his dad completely self-destruct. It's a sad thing. As a child, I watched my father do the same; destroy himself.

Addiction has plagued the men of my family for over 3 generations. Recently though, I learned about this generational curse. I learned the only way to break these chains is to grab ahold of Jesus Christ and never let go.

One of the hardest things for me in beating these poor choices that I've made is built on self-condemnation for the bad decisions.

2 Corinthians 5:17 says,

Therefore if anyone is in Christ, he is a new creature and all things have passed away, and all things have become new.

That's what it's all about.

I don't have to be tangled up in that bondage any longer. Jesus went to the cross and took care of that for me. He made me feel worthy again. And it's an awesome feeling to know that Jesus Christ has my back no matter what. I know that if I keep Jesus number one in my life, all things will fall into place. If I go back to try to take control; put myself before Christ, the inevitable will happen.

This is the most important thing that I have learned: Go through Jesus Christ for all of the decisions that I make for my future. If I couldn't control my life, and no one else could, what else is left but to trust precious Jesus?

Isaiah 1:19 says that,

If you are willing and obedient to His Word, you shall eat the good of the land.

That tells me that if I am obedient to the Lord's Word, I am going to receive all of the things this world has to offer. Better yet, what the Kingdom has to offer.

At this time, I would like to say; Mom, I've put you through so much. You've never given up on me. That is truly unconditional love. I love you, and Happy Mother's Day. Crystal, you've done an awesome job raising our son and I appreciate you. God couldn't have given our son a better mother. I love you. Happy Mother's Day!

I'm going to take a second and tell these guys in my class with me, thank you guys! I will never forget you. We've been through so much together, and I wish you guys the best. Faith Farm staff, I would like to thank you so very much for helping me to turn my life around. Thank you for Class 5 and for helping me open up some issues that needed to be addressed.

In closing, I would like to say to all my brothers here, Jesus has changed my life, one hundred percent. When I got here, I was a lost soul looking for help. I had to fully surrender and tell myself to put it in Jesus' hands. He has taken control of my life, and He has worked miracles. He will do the same for you guys. I love you guys.

Brenda

First and foremost, I want to give all the glory to my Lord and Savior, Jesus Christ. Because of Him, I am standing here in front of you today to testify about how He has influenced me and saved me from my mess.

I want to let you know a little bit about where I come from, how I came to Faith Farm and where the Lord has taken me. I was born and raised in Queens, New York. I was raised into an environment full of chaos. I was a witness to sex, drugs and abuse at a very young age, and then later became a victim of it.

My father played a very big role in abuse towards my mother and me. By the time I was 7, my parents had divorced. Although I love my father, I was happy to be free from his abuse. That happiness quickly faded, and sadness and depression quickly became part of my life. Not only did I lose a father, but I had an absent mother. So much of my childhood was spent with babysitters or other family members that I never got to build the true, mother-daughter relationship that I wanted and needed.

I decided to go live with my father when I was 10. He had remarried and seemed to have changed from his abusive ways. I was so desperately seeking some stability of what a family life should be for me. I was wrong. My father still abused drugs and then he abused me. By this time, I was experimenting a lot with marijuana. This allowed me to mask my pain and escape from my life, not to mention I thought it was the cool thing to do with my friends.

By the time I was 13, my father threw me out of my home and into the streets. I began hanging out with gang members, and most of them were drug dealers. Before I knew it, I was selling drugs for them.

I had quickly learned how to be a survivor of the street life. I'm not proud of the things I did, but at that time, I had no real guidance or stability. I did not have a relationship with God. I knew of a God just because I was told there was one. I did not truly know Him, and my life was full of sin.

By the time I was 15, my life had another big change. My mom found out I was no longer with my dad. Somehow through the courts, she was awarded custody of me and had me brought to Florida where she resided.

Things were rough for my mother. Five years had passed without really knowing each other, especially throughout the most important years of my life. It also didn't help that my mother's boyfriend, who I did not like, was in the picture trying to play the father role. It was because of him that my mother and I argued a lot. This led to a big fight between us one day, and I did the unthinkable; I hit my mother numerous times. The next thing I knew, I'm being thrown out of the house again. This just brought me into a bigger depression in my life. I felt nobody loved me nor wanted me.

I moved in with my boyfriend; living the "adult life." I began experimenting with acid and rolls. Life in those days was great and full of happiness, or so I thought. Because of my partying ways, I was out of control and even abusive towards my boyfriend. So he left me.

I continued to hide my pain. I just did more drugs and jumped into another relationship. After 4 months of dating, we got married. Things were great at first, as they always are, but I was living a life of lies. I learned I was pregnant. I was so excited to think of being a mom. Finally, I thought, I have something worth living for. I was about to have something I could love that would love me back, even with all of my flaws. That excitement and joy quickly faded away on my 21st birthday, which I spent in the hospital being told by doctors that I had miscarried.

I went deeper into drugs when I lost my twins. I felt as if I was being punished for all the wrong things I had done in the past. I wanted children so badly that I agreed to have the surgery that doctors told me I needed in order to have children. Without a second thought, or opinion, I put all my trust into the doctors and had the surgery. This was a big mistake. My surgery went terribly wrong. In the process of my surgery, the doctors cut my bladder extensively, and I was stuck in ICU for a week or two. I went through 6 painful surgeries in 8 months to reconstruct my bladder. Within this span of time I had a failed marriage, lost my teaching job, quit school and fell into a deep depression that I hid through the numerous painkillers given to me by my doctors. I was only 22 when all of this happened to me.

From that moment until I arrived at Faith Farm, it was just one big roller coaster. I went through a few more relationships, lost some more jobs, and my drug habit got worse. Due to my drug habit, I began to isolate myself from my family and friends. I was so ashamed and embarrassed over what I had become, which was an addict. I could not face my family, and my pride did not allow me to admit I had a problem. I convinced myself, "I got this; I can beat this addiction." There goes my pride.

My mom tried to help me, but my stubbornness and denial did not allow it. The devil sure did have that stronghold on me. I finally did speak to my mom about getting help, and she introduced me to Faith Farm. At first, I was OK in trying this place because I thought it was just some regular rehab center. Then she mentions it's a faith-based program. I quickly put the brakes on that conversation. That was completely different from what I had in mind. I did not know just then that this was all in God's plan for me.

The way my mind worked, I thought I was entering some sort of convent. I mean, I had never even read a Bible before. Now, my mom wants me to go to some faith-based program? It was very easy for me to decline my mom's offer. The devil did not want me going, and at that moment, he won! Therefore, I continued to do what I always did, get high. About 4 months later while on my way to work, I was high. I don't know what came over me, but I had enough of the way I was living. It was at that moment I quit my job, called my mom and said, "I'm ready! Let's do this." On November 23rd of last year, I came to Faith Farm.

Philippians 3:8 states,

> *All things are worth nothing compared to knowing Christ Jesus my Lord.*

Faith Farm has taught me this. I never knew much of Jesus or how to build a relationship with Him. I couldn't forgive myself for all the pain I've caused, and I wondered how He could forgive me. Then He told me in Jeremiah 31:34,

> *I will forgive their inequity and their sin I will remember no more.*

Once I truly believed this, the Lord began opening my eyes and began breaking down my walls.

Then the Lord spoke to me again in Romans 6:12-14:

> *Therefore, do not let sin reign in your mortal body so you obey its evil desires. Do not offer parts of your body to sin as instruments of its wickedness, but offer yourselves to God as those who have been brought*

190

from dead to life. Offer all parts of your body to Him as instruments of righteousness, for sin will not be your master if you are not under law, but you are under grace.

It was at this very moment that I wanted to give my all to Christ.

On January 12th of this year, I was baptized. It was the greatest feeling ever. I felt like a new creature in Christ. I never thought I could experience such joy and freedom as I have experienced here at Faith Farm. The Lord has blessed me in so many ways. He has delivered me from drugs, and He has given me hope and faith, which has allowed me to experience this awesome relationship with Him. And the best blessing; He has given me restoration with my mother and family.

God is good everybody; God is good. I love you all, and I thank you so much for the support you have given me throughout this whole process. I love you so much, Mom. You are my rock, and I love you. Thank God, He brought us back together again.

Lynne

Good Morning, Church. I am the 5th of 6 children in my family. We were all raised in the Catholic religion. My brothers, sisters and I were baptized as infants, attended Catholic grade school and went to church every Sunday. We said our prayers before meals and bedtime, and we were taught to obey the Ten Commandments. We knew about the Father, Son and Holy Spirit. But, I do not remember reading a Bible during my childhood or even owning one. During Mass, the priests would read scriptures and then give their sermons. Most of the time, I had no idea what they were speaking about. That, in a nut shell, is what I knew about religion.

My adult life seemed to be normal enough. I married and had 2 children. About 5 years ago, I was in a car accident that changed everything. My recovery was long, hard and difficult. During that time I turned to alcohol. It was an addiction that engulfed my life. Everything was out of control. Sadly, my marriage ended, and I lost just about everything, including the trust of my family. But most important, I hurt the ones I loved dearly.

I decided to come to Faith Farm for help with my addiction. I was angry, lonely, desperate and depressed. That was January of last year. I did not give anyone or anything here a chance. I thought someone else deserved my bed more than I did, so I left. Then several months after leaving, I finally got the courage to pick up the phone and humble myself for another chance.

I thought it would be the most difficult phone call I would ever make. But, Sister Paula made it the easiest call I ever made. That was the first step to making my life right.

When I came back, I knew that somehow I had to make this work. People kept telling me about how you can have a personal relationship with God. I had no idea what they were talking about. I thought – how is that possible? This is **GOD** we're talking about. That just doesn't happen: **GOD,** the Creator of Heaven and Earth. They told me to read His Word, to read the Bible and then read it again. Do it with an open heart and open mind. And to my surprise, I found that His Word didn't wear out.

They also said to spend quiet time with God. I decided the only way to really have quiet time with Him was to be alone, and that's not an easy thing to do around here. So I started walking in the field behind the women's home as often as I could. At first, all I did was complain, but that did not get me anywhere. Then I made the argument that it's not right. This should not be happening to me. That didn't work either.

At some point, I stopped complaining and started talking. I did a lot of walking and talking and praying. I realized He was listening to me and answering me. I found this relationship to be possible because He gave His only son, Jesus, for me. I was making something so difficult that really is so simple – if you truly want it.

I have found the joy of the Lord in my heart. Psalms 34:4 tells us,

> Take delight in the Lord and he will give you your hearts desires.

I know now He is always there. He will help you if you ask. He will never leave you. He is a loving and merciful God. 1 Peter 5:7 says,

> Give all your worries and cares to God, for He cares for you.

Remember that there is always hope, help and a way to overcome. I do know this ministry saves lives through the power of the Holy Spirit, and I will be forever grateful. Just be still and patient and watch what God does when you truly trust Him and walk by faith.

I would like to thank the staff and leaders of the women's home. Thank you for all that you have done for me. You will always be in my heart. I love you all.

I would like to close with a verse that always brings me hope when I think there isn't any to be found. You can find it in the Book of Psalms.

Give thanks to the Lord, for He is good. His faithful love endures forever.

Thank you.

Gracie

My name is Sharee Grace, affectionately known as Gracie. I was born in Philadelphia, Pennsylvania. My parents were not married. My mother was 21 and already on her 3rd child. All I knew of my father was that he was a man who came and left, A LOT.

The early years of my life were spent following behind my mother and her big red suitcase from place to place, until we finally settled into our 3 bedroom house in the middle of north Philadelphia. My mother needed help paying rent, so when I was 5 years old, she opened her home to my aunt and her 3 little girls. This is when I was first introduced to Satan.

My mother would work long days and we would stay home with my aunt. My young eyes witnessed brutal beatings, hands being burned on the stove and bloody knees that came from kneeling for hours on raw grits. And, when she was at her most hideous, my mother and I would come home to find one of my cousins wedged in-between the screen and storm doors desperately trying to hide herself after she'd been forced outside completely naked and the door locked behind her. I couldn't understand my mother's indifference. My heart cried out in agony for them. I would throw myself over my cousins, kick and claw my aunt. At times, I would just try and plead with her. I remember feeling so powerless and guilty that nothing ever happened to me. My mother eventually asked her to leave.

When I was 7 years old, I was introduced to Jesus. In my neighborhood, the little corner and storefront churches had the giant speakers sitting right outside on full blast for anyone who thought they'd be sleeping in that morning. You were coming to church

197

whether you liked it or not. I remember the beautiful voice of the woman in the choir singing about how much Jesus loved me. I followed that voice; that pull on my little spirit, into the church. I started going to the Christians Reaching Youth, or C.R.Y. program, on Monday nights to learn about Jesus. My mother was never a religious woman, but she didn't seem to object to my interest.

I know now that my Father in Heaven was stepping in for my absentee father by educating me about His love and the strength and power of His protection. As Paul says in Romans 8:16,

His Holy Spirit speaks to us deep in our hearts and tells us that we are God's children.

He let me know then that I was precious; the apple of His eye, and I had His love no matter what. He also knew I wouldn't be able to protect myself from what was coming for me. A few short months after starting Bible classes, I was reunited with Satan in the form of sexual abuse. My world was shattered, and my soul was torn. My mother walked in on the abuse one night. I thought my troubles were over. But she didn't move an inch as he fled the room. Then she turned her eyes on me. Suddenly, she flew at me, and I was pinned against the wall by my throat. She kept screaming, "How could you let him do that to you?" It was then branded into my mind that if I wasn't so powerless, I could have stopped him. I stopped going to church after that. I could not get past the shame that was threatening to bring me to tears at even the slightest display of affection. I didn't want the little clean and pure girls hugging me. But most of all, I did not want to hate them for their beautiful innocence.

A year later, my mother found out she was pregnant by her current boyfriend and that we were moving to a better neighborhood. I had hoped that this would mean a brand new start. My little sister was such a blessing. She was instantly attached to me and made me feel so loved and so good. I can see now the way the Lord was trying to remind me; He was still there by my side. But the gaping wound that was once a housing place for my spirit was filling quickly with hate, rejection and rage. I began acting out. By the age of 11, I was lashing out violently, smoking cigarettes and pot, drinking and staying out until early morning, if I came home at all.

My mother began her career as a bartender and decided she could no longer handle my behavior. She made the decision that it was in my best interest to go and live with the stranger, also known as my father. There, I was only met with more neglect from my father and physical, mental and emotional abuse from his wife. Unbeknownst to me, she had been trying for some time to conceive, but to no avail. I, apparently, was a constant reminder that another woman could give her husband children and she could not, and for that I paid a severe price.

The next 8 years of my life were a blur of fighting, running away, group homes, promiscuity, experimental drugs, alcohol, parties and any other form of debauchery I could sink into. I had no fear. I despised weakness and I ignored God.

My best friend, Loreal, was always trying to bring me back to the Lord. It was by God's divine appointment that we met, and we became closer than sisters almost immediately. Loreal ignited the spark that would catch ablaze, melt my cold heart and eventually lead me back into the arms of Jesus.

I found myself on a plane for the first time in my life last July, when on my way to Florida. I was sure it was going to be the best move I have ever made. Up until then, I was selling drugs to get drugs, and I hated myself for it. No matter what I did, I could not get from under this smothering pillow of depression.

2 Corinthians 7:10 tell us of

> ... A godly grief that produces repentance that leads to salvation.

I had been stalking Sister Paula for 2 months, calling her everyday. I even left her messages with Sister Di when she specifically told me she'd be away on vacation. I was either waiting for her to give me the green light or for death to run me down. But God had a bigger plan for me than I ever had for myself. Isaiah 43 is my favorite chapter in the Bible. In it, the Lord told me that, not if but,

> *When I pass through the waters, He will be with me, and when I pass through the rivers they will not sweep over me. When I walk through the fire, I will not be burned: the flames will not set me ablaze; for He is the Lord My God, the Holy One of Israel, my Savior.*

My life has been saved here. I have been reconciled to my Abba. My soul has been mended with the pouring out of healing from the Father through his servants.

During a recent visit home, I was confronted by a family member who is an unbeliever. She said, "Sharee, how can you say God loves You? You've been through hell. You've been beaten, misused, rejected and betrayed. The man, who was supposed to lead, guide and protect you, abandoned you, not once ... but time and time again. The woman who was supposed to teach and nurture you, guard your life with a fierce natural prowess, left you vulnerable to the worst kind of predators. How can you call that love? How does that make any sense?"

Simply because God wins no ultimate victory except through the grave of apparent defeat!

Like My Savior, Jesus, my purpose was to suffer. Suffer and die to myself so I can be redeemed by the blood of the Lamb, overcome by His magnificent loving strength and show others the way home. I have been given the unimaginable honor of being a beacon of hope and bringing Glory to the King of Kings and the unmatchable joy that comes with living in the light of His Favor.

My favorite chapter went on to tell me, and He would have me say this to you,

> *Forget the former things; do not dwell on the past. See, I am doing a new thing! Now it springs up; do you not perceive it? I am making a way in the desert and streams in the wasteland.*

Thank You and God Bless.

Cindy

Good morning, Church. What an exciting journey this has been! I can honestly say that Faith Farm was not what I was expecting. Looking back in my journal, the second day I was here I wrote, "I would be a fool not to take this incredible opportunity to begin a new life. I liked myself sober before. I want myself back."

For a long time, I've been trying to figure out what I kept missing. What's really been going on in my life that makes me relapse? That first week, I was blessed to hear Beth Moore speak. Psalms 37:4-5 says,

> Take delight in the Lord and He will give you your heart's desire. Commit everything you do to the Lord. Trust Him and He will help you.

I realized that it's exactly what I needed to hear. I began to pray and ask God to make my heart's desire God's desire for my heart. Instead of asking Him to give me what I wanted, I needed to ask Him to show me what He wanted.

Proverbs 3:5-6 says,

> Trust in the Lord with all your heart and do not depend on your own understanding. Seek His will in all you do and He will show you which path to take.

I never really read the Bible until I got here. When my mom gave me the *Life Recovery Bible,* I can't begin to tell you how much it made the Word come alive and make sense to me.

On November 8th, Pastor preached on Romans 7 and struggling with sin.

Romans 15 states,

> *I don't really understand myself, for I want to do what is right, but I don't do it. Instead I do what I hate.*

My picture should be next to that verse!

Then I went on to read in Romans 8:6,

> *So letting your sinful nature control your mind leads to death. But letting the Spirit control your mind leads to life and peace.*

I began to realize why this is a 9 month or more program. We've all heard the expression, "What would Jesus do?" Then I heard someone say, "What would Jesus think?" What would Jesus want me to think? Romans 12:2 states,

> *Let God transform you into a new person by changing the way you think.*

Proverbs 2:2-3 states,

> *Tune your ears to wisdom and concentrate on understanding. Cry out for insight and ask for understanding.*

James 1:5 states,

> *If you need wisdom ask our generous God and He will give it to you.*

This takes time. He's not finished with me yet. These last 9 months have flown by for me. I plan on staying as an extended student. My job has and will continue to be baking. They say a good cook doesn't follow a recipe. Well … let me tell you, when you don't have all the right ingredients your bread won't rise!

I've found the missing ingredient in my life. It's all right in here! Romans 8:28 states,

> And we know that God causes everything to work together for the good of those who love God and are called according to His purpose for them.

My mom tried to get me to Faith Farm back in 1999. How I wish I had listened. James 4:8 states,

> Come close to God and God will come close to you.

I'd like to close with Romans 8:38-39,

> And I am convinced that nothing can ever separate us from God's love. Neither death nor life; neither angels nor demons; neither our fears for today nor our worries about tomorrow; not even the powers of hell can separate us from God's love. No power in the sky above or in the earth below, indeed, nothing in all creation will ever be able to separate us from the love of God that is revealed in Christ Jesus our Lord.

Tara

I am writing this testimony as a praise offering to Jesus Christ for the love He gave a sinner like me, and for bringing me out of all the hell I was living in. I have realized that His love has always been with me, even when I did not know it.

My name is Tara. I was born October 31, 1974, in a small town outside of Atlanta, Georgia, called Newnan. I was given to my great-great grandparents at the tender age of 2 days old. I was raised in a Baptist church. Although I was taught about Jesus, I did not have a personal relationship with Him. My grandfather went home to live with the Lord when I was 9 years old and my grandmother, bless her heart, just now turned 98 years young! They were the only parents I knew, and I loved them dearly.

Growing up, I would always wonder where I came from because all my grandparents' children were much older than me. At 10 years old, I learned that my birth mother was alive and lived within miles of where I lived. Within one year, I moved in with her. With that move came a drastic change to the life I had known. I had no idea what I was in for. This is when I was exposed to drugs, making fast money, mental, emotional, physical and sexual abuse.

At the age of 11, I was raped for the first time by a very close family member and drug dealer. During these years of my life, where most girls are learning and growing into young ladies, I was subject to a lifestyle of abandonment, abuse and rape. Not until much later in my life did I realize the huge effect this would have on the lifestyle and choices I would make as an adult.

When I was 16, I came home from school to find my mother gone. After speaking with my aunt, I was told she would not return.

207

This is when my aunt allowed me to live with her and her 3 children. While working and going to school full-time, I discovered I was 6 weeks pregnant by my boyfriend of 2 years. I thought this would change him, make him happy and draw him closer to me. Boy, was I wrong! He still wanted to live his life and have more than one girlfriend, so I called it quits and had my daughter on my own.

At the age of 19, my daughter and I moved to Florida. During this time, I met my first husband. This was the most abusive and toxic relationship of my life. When I was age 20, I had my son. At 23, I had my second daughter. The abuse continued throughout this whole time. In 2001, while walking to the courthouse to file for my divorce, my husband hit me from behind with a truck! And now, I will have to live the rest of my life with an injury and memories that constantly remind me of the day my life was almost taken. Many people would ask me why I stayed so long. The only answer I could come up with was, "I was too scared to leave."

It got to the point where I decided to trust God instead of dwelling on my fears, and I finally filed for my divorce and a permanent restraining order that is still in place today. Psalm 34:4 states,

> I sought the lord, and he heard me, and delivered me
> from all my fears. (NIV)

I spent the next few years as a single mother raising 3 children, working and going to school full-time to obtain my LPN license. During this time, I met the man that would later become my current husband.

After being prescribed pain pills at the age of 25, I used for the first time. I had no idea what I was in for and how these pills that were prescribed to me because of an accident would change my life. I

208

took them as prescribed for a few years, but then the real addiction set in while I was working as a nurse. I started writing my own scripts by taking the prescription pads from work and cutting out my doctor visits all together. My family and friends had no idea what was going on with me.

I was tired of acting free when I was not. I was tired of acting strong, when in fact, I was weak.

In 2002, I was arrested for the first time for attempting to obtain a controlled substance by fraud. I was put on 4 years' probation. By the grace of God, I got through it successfully. In 2007, I was arrested for the second time, with a long list of charges. I was charged with 2 counts of trafficking in oxycodone, 47 counts of Rx fraud, fleeing and alluding, giving a false name; all while driving on a suspended license. Needless to say, I was highly intoxicated. I share this to show you just where my addiction took me. After sitting in jail for 7 months facing a 25-year mandatory sentence, I saw God's grace and mercy first hand. Forty-five counts of Rx fraud were dropped. My final sentence was 10 years drug offender probation and a 10-month program with Palm Beach Drug Farm, which was a boot camp, military style! O...M...G! I don't know how I survived that one! That was followed by 4 months at a halfway house and 2 months aftercare. I completed everything and remained clean.

Due to all this, there was no work available for me in the medical field, so I was hired as a call center supervisor. It was there that I relapsed when I was introduced to the little blue devils . . . roxies! I went from taking them to selling them. I enjoyed the lifestyle I grew up in, knowing as a child about making fast money. But, like I was always told fast money does not last long. And it did not.

I started using more than I sold. I guess you can say I became my number one customer. I fell into a very deep depression and gave up all hope. I lost my job and my children were rebelling. I lost my apartment. You name it, it happened. I felt trapped by my past … yet afraid of my future. I was stepping forward while always looking back. When I came to the end of my own strength is when I found God's strength.

2 Corinthians 12:9 states,

> My grace is all you need; my power works best in weakness. (NIV)

I am glad to boast in my weakness, so that the power of Christ can work through me.

I called my probation officer and told him I was struggling; that my addiction was starting to take control of me again. He advised me to go get help. So, I checked myself into detox for 7 days. When I called him to advise him I was in detox, I learned he had violated me for not checking in. There was a warrant issued for my arrest. The night of Thanksgiving 2011, while with my cousin, we got pulled over. Back to jail I went. I did 65 days, saw the judge 4 times and was denied bond, house arrest and community control. Because of my violations, they wanted me to do my full 25 year sentence. I started praying, as did my family, friends and church family.

It was in jail that God got my attention once again. The fear that I might be going to prison and lose my family was overwhelming. During the days that followed, God began to speak to me. He gave me the opportunity to return back to Him. I was completely broken and had nowhere to go but to Him. I made the decision there in jail to turn away from sin. I knew God had a bigger purpose for my life. I started praying that He would keep me out of prison, give me the help I needed and keep my family together. God once again showed His love, mercy and favor. He heard my cry and answered my prayers.

I was given time served and the court ordered me to Faith Farm for a 9-month program.

I arrived here at Faith Farm on January 31, 2012. The 9 months I have been here have not been easy, but they have been well worth it. I have been put to the test, to say the least. I had to deal with and overcome hurt, disappointments, being misled and misunderstood. Romans 8:28 states:

> We know that all things work together for good to those who love God, to those who are called according to his purpose.

I finally had to turn the hurts of my life over to God's sovereign authority. If not, it would consume me like cancer. I am finally surrendering my past, present and future to Him. Through this, not only did God give me peace, but He showed me how good can be brought from something so horrible and unfair.

Genesis 50:20 tells me,

> You intended to harm me, but God intended it for good to accomplish what is now being done, the saving of many lives.

Glory be to God, who has turned my life, which was once a test, into my testimony. Thank you, Father God, for giving me the challenges that brought me to my knees.

Britt

I always thought I was in control of my own life. I figured the choices I made and the direction I steered my life would determine the value and success in my life. It took me 22 years to realize that there is so much more to life than what I had in mind.

I was born on February 20, 1990, to 2 loving parents. Growing up, I strived to be a good student and did my best to honor my parent's rules and restrictions. They instilled in me good morals and values, but something inside of me was always drawn to a life of sin.

Once I hit my teenage years, my rebellious spirit began to show itself slowly, but surely. By high school, I was drinking and smoking pot at parties on the weekends. I loved being the life of the party. To me, there was nothing wrong with just having a little fun. Throughout my high school years, I became increasingly more curious and began experimenting with a wide variety of drugs. I started taking whatever was available, as long as it would get me high. In my mind, I wasn't addicted to anything. It was just fun for me. I simply liked to get high! Everybody does. There's no harm in it, right?

Little did I know, I was steadily spiraling downward to rock bottom! I was only a "party girl" until I tried that infamous little blue pill; a roxy. That little blue pill sent me over the edge, from recreational user to "I have a drug problem!" As my using pattern progressed, completely unaware at the time, I was steadily morphing into a very warped version of myself. Before I knew it, I was acting out in ways that were totally contrary to my life long values. Fortunately, my family intervened and confronted me with truth and reality. I was very much in denial, so hearing my family's opinions was an eye opening experience of what I had become. The next day, I was at

Faith Farm and four hours away from anything remotely familiar to me.

Initially, everything was very foreign to me. I was a professed atheist, so I was SO not into all this "God stuff." To me, everyone was weird, and I was miserable. I had little interest in getting to know God. All I knew was I couldn't stand the way I was living and I couldn't stand myself. So, my cry to the Lord started out as an act of desperation. But as time went on, I started to feel an indescribable presence that I knew was not of this earth. Throughout the next few months, I increasingly became more curious and hungry for the Lord. The hungrier I got, the more I sought the Lord, and He was faithful in filling me up.

I steadily acquired a conviction and a desire for the Lord I never knew. I no longer saw Jesus as a character in the Bible, but as Lord, Savior, and most of all a friend. Romans 8:28 says,

> *All things work together for good to those who love God and to those who are called according to His purpose.*

If I never became addicted to drugs, I never would have come to Faith Farm and possibly never would have come to the Lord. Now, I can honestly say that I have peace though my trials, because I know God has a plan for my life. He is refining me, like gold is refined in the fire. If you can learn to walk by faith and trust His immeasurable understanding, He can exceed beyond anything you could ever imagine or hope for.

For a long time, I struggled with forgiving myself for the horrible things my addiction led me to do to my loved ones. Not forgiving myself only led me deeper into my depression. So, I continued to act out in destructive ways. The Lord has shown me that if He can forgive me. I can forgive me. Although I am still working on forgiving myself, I have started to experience the freedom of Christ and the relief of giving these bondages to Jesus.

I'd like to say thank you to my family. Thank you for never giving up on me and loving me no matter what. I wouldn't be standing up here today if it wasn't for the genuine love from the staff here. Sister Paula, Sister Ann, Sister Diane, Sister Gail, Heidi and Marrion: I want to thank all of you for everything you do for this program. You have each had an individual impact on my recovery. I love you guys! I came here broken and stubborn, with no faith and no hope. But I'm graduating today filled up with the love and peace, with a newfound faith in Jesus Christ and I will serve Him forever! Thank you.

Richard

Author's Note: *Eighteen years ago, Richard "crawled" (as he puts it) through the front entry gate of the Ft. Lauderdale, Faith Farm campus. He absorbed the program materials, especially the parts about building a personal relationship with God, and excelled at every department he was placed to work. He eventually became the director over the entire Ft. Lauderdale campus program. He is an example to the men in the program, showing that all things are possible. He's a reminder that it's how you finish that people remember your life.*

As a child, I was very fortunate to be surrounded by family who truly loved and cared for me. My parents were not famous or wealthy, though they were honest, respectful and compassionate. Our financial status would be considered in the middle-upper class. We were always taken care of, but that is not what stands out to me. I knew whenever I needed to talk to my dad; he would always give me good, sound advice. He always said, "No question is stupid; it's stupid not to ask."

My dad was very compassionate and understanding, but at the same time, "no" meant "no"! He did not tolerate disobedience and rebellion. My childhood upbringing helped me to walk the straight and narrow.

I didn't smoke, drink or use drugs until I enlisted in the Marines. I started drinking, but it didn't get out of control until much later in life. After about 6 months of intense combat training, I was given orders for Vietnam. I had no idea what would transpire in the next year. My life had become extremely stressful, and I came to the realization that marijuana masked the problems I was going through in the midst of a war, to which I had been subjected.

While in Vietnam, I received two Purple Hearts for wounds received in combat. The second was a severe wound that introduced me to a wonderful feeling of euphoria from Demerol, a narcotic painkiller. Being hospitalized in Yokohama, Japan, I became addicted to the medication. After I was released from the hospital, I stopped the heavier drugs but continued the use of marijuana.

Once I was released from the Marines, I decided to move to California, and I gradually stopped all use of drugs including cigarettes. At that time, I was not a Christian, but I did possess a strong sense of will-power. I remember one day just strolling on the beach and saying to myself, "Why waste my time jogging on the beach and working out just to destroy my body with drugs and cigarettes?" At that point, I stopped all of those habits and focused on a healthy and productive lifestyle.

In 1975, after having my first real encounter with Christ, I met the woman that would become my first wife. We married about a year later, and I thought she was the woman God had for me. We seemed to be happily married, but as I look back, I don't believe I was truly in love. Knowing God's will about divorce, I said that would never be an option. So, with that in mind we remained together for 16 years. We started our partnership with a lot of obstacles to overcome, but finally, we were able to work most of them out over time.

In the beginning of our marriage, we worked for the same company. She worked as the executive secretary, and I was a mechanical draftsman. We worked there for about 2 years, until the company went bankrupt. I became a proficient machinist while there, which later would become a great asset to me.

I was interested in working for Lockheed Aeronautical Systems (Lockheed Martin) due to their excellent salary and benefit package. I filled out an application for the job I desired, but I was willing to take whatever was available. Why not, considering that their lowest paying job was starting at $8.00 an hour? In1977, that was an excellent wage for someone to clean machine parts, and I would be getting my foot in the door.

I was hired as a machinist and quickly advanced to a CNC programmer, aircraft inspector and subsequently, to management. I was always dedicated to my work and the job went well until the work became my God, even over my family. I began to work 50 hours a week routinely and often on Sundays. This left out any time for family life. Even worse, a deep deficit formed in my relationship I had with Christ, not that I ever had a solid foundation in the first place.

Our marriage after 15 years was shattered. I had no interest in her, and she had no interest in me. This was affecting my work to the point I had to see a doctor for anxiety and panic disorder. I could no longer handle the pressure of work, which was very demanding on the marriage. I finally decided to resign from Lockheed after 12 years of service, and it wasn't long after that I started to drink. I had stopped taking the medication for anxiety disorder and just substituted alcohol for it. The drinking became a lifestyle; I didn't work or really do anything productive. I lived off my savings and 401(k) until I could no longer make the mortgage payments.

I ended up selling the house and moving to Virginia to live with my mother. I thought a geographical change would help change my condition. I learned that moving to a new environment would not solve the crisis. When I got there, there I was! I was the problem, but I was not yet able to figure this out. I was sober for about a month. But as soon as I became employed, it was over. I had a party to celebrate as soon as I was paid, and the drinking cycle started again.

I came up with another brilliant idea; if I went back to my roots, maybe there might be hope. Once again, I was wrong. I found a job in Davie, Florida, as a mechanical inspector and started making a decent salary. I remember it like yesterday. I was happy, celebrating about 6 months of sobriety, and I just bought a new car. I thought, I'll stop at the 7-11 on the way home from work just to get a cold tea or something. When I went into the store, a can of cold beer looked me straight in the face, and it was all over.

I decided, with the help of my sister, to be admitted to a program. My sister was familiar with Salvation Army, and I was in need of salvation!

I went to the program out of desperation, not knowing what to expect, but hoping it would be the answer to my long desired deliverance. After 6 months, I found myself in the same dilemma; missing something deep inside that could not be fixed through religion or a program. There was still a missing link between real sobriety and just staying clean. Yes, I was sober, but I had no tranquility within. I still felt that life was not worth living. I would have committed suicide if I had the guts, but I could not bring myself to that point, even though I thought of it many times. Before I checked out of Salvation Army's program, someone there mentioned Faith Farm. He told me that Faith Farm was similar to the Salvation Army's program, but more strict and fanatical.

After leaving Salvation Army, I thought a lot about Faith Farm and what he had said. Maybe that's what I needed, even though it wasn't what I wanted. I wasn't drinking, but like I said earlier, I was a sober drunk; totally disgusted, busted and disconnected with life.

After living with my sister for several months and her getting to the point of telling me to get some help or get out, I decided to give Faith Farm a chance. I had tried everything else and absolutely nothing worked for me, so why not? I called and was placed on a waiting list for about 2 weeks, which seemed like an eternity. Finally,

I was asked to come in and fill out an application. That very day I was accepted in the program.

Faith Farm turned out to be much different than I had imagined. I thought it was just another religious program. After a couple days, I realized there was definitely something different. I came to understand it was the presence of the Holy Spirit. I made the decision to give Faith Farm an opportunity to change my life. I became conscious of an inner peace once I made that decision. I was blessed after several months in the program to be assigned to the church as the custodian. That was where the growth in my life began to blossom. I realized that prayer and a solid commitment to the Holy Spirit was the answer I had been seeking. People like Stu, and others of his spirit, made a significant impact in my life from the time I entered the program, even up to this day.

One thing I became conscience of right from the start; there were people here who were sincerely interested in me and wanted me to enter into the transformed life that God had for me. Through the years, I have managed many departments at Faith Farm, eventually becoming Campus Director. Without His grace, it would all have been a trivial and meaningless journey.

There have been many changes in my life since the day I walked in the gates of the Ft. Lauderdale Faith Farm Ministries. I've truly been blessed! God even gave me a second chance in marriage. I now know what marriage is really meant to be in God's sight. He has given me a helpmate that places her relationship with Jesus Christ above all others.

Faith Farm is an amazing and magnificent tool that God uses to transform men and women from a life of hopelessness to hope and depression to living a life of freedom. The Bible says we can do all things through Christ.

I thank God for the privilege of serving Him in a manner that is not only rewarding to me, but is changing lives like mine into people that make a difference to a hurting and dying world. As Faith Farm Ministries motto declares, we truly are "A Ministry with a Heart for the Hurting." One thing for sure, it's been quite a journey.

Angelique

The relationship I have now with the Lord wasn't always so. My relationship with God was quid pro quo. "God I promise I will ... if you would just ..." I had no knowledge of the authority that The Almighty possessed in my life. I did not grow up on a foundation of mindfulness for The Word. I was easily deceived, and therefore, subject to misfortunes by my own actions.

The evil one's endeavors yoked my thoughts and flesh. As he triumphed over my gullibility, I became further from God's fruit and closer to the devil's devouring. He was like a black widow in my ear spouting poison and making webs; catching all words of good and storing them up to feast on them so that I may never know truth. He used his venom to deafen my eardrums. The toxins circulated to my heart causing it to harden and my soul give-way. Where, you may ask, was my soul going? It was going to a place far worse than that of the somber of death.

In my times of despair, I felt as though God did not and would not see me. I felt like mere nothingness. I believed that God did not love me ... He was not an all-benevolent and virtuous Lord. How could God be good in all entireties if He did not love me? With that, I relinquished, wallowing in the abysmal darkness for many sullen years. All the while feeling alone and inadequate, I believed my feelings to be true. The untruths were just fallacies kidnapping me from my Savior. The more pregnable I felt, the more I became the lies. I believed my circumstances would never change.

Being deceived by Satan is like being at the beach. There you are on a sunny clear day splashing around in the water. Caught up in the fun, you become unaware of your surroundings. You drift further and further from where you were and from whom you were with. Before you realize it, you don't recognize where you are anymore. Frantically, amongst the chaos, you look for familiarities. In your distress, a wave comes unexpectedly, knocks you off your feet and pulls you under.

It was in those onyx moments I cried out to the Lord; the crucial time where I believed I could take no more. Ten days later, I arrived at Faith Farm. All the suffering and all the years of anguish, the devil never gave me what God gave me within 10 days by just calling on His Name once. My surrender saved my life. Like our Father sacrificed His son for our sins, I yielded my son for my own sins. It was a minute offering to establish concrete truth. The innocence opened again to claim my innocence.

This sanctuary and its ordained vessels transformed me. It made me realize I was trapped in my very own cage built for me and by me. Even when the cage door was wide open, I returned to it like a carrier pigeon does his coop; except now, I no longer carry advertisements from Satan, but messages from God.

God has abounding love. His probity is sovereign. His hand will guide my circumstances if my will allows it. My feelings are just fleeting inklings that are like clay. I chose my potter. I will only be sculptured by the Lord, my God.

God instills in you a heart that holds 4 chambers. In 3 of the chambers reside The Father, The Son, and The Holy Spirit. In the fourth chamber, you yourself reside. Your own self is only one quarter of the image God has created you in; a small fraction of infarction; an insignificant, meager part of you that withers away. It's the parts that are paramount, that are internal and that are eternal that have significance.

Ricardo

I was born in Buenos Aires, Argentina. I am the oldest child with 2 younger brothers and a sister. Growing up, my family moved a great deal. We lived in South America, Australia, England, and Canada. We moved to the United States, where we lived in Pennsylvania before I entered my teen years. Growing up, I had terrific parents that raised me in a caring, Christian environment. My father is a pastor. So, my upbringing was quite strict, but loving as well.

During my senior year of high school, I began to look at different schools to attend college. It was early February and I decided to visit a school in West Palm Beach, Florida. I noticed the bright blue sky, warm weather and the blue water at the beach. I decided that this school probably had the best academic curriculum for me.

After graduating high school, I came to South Florida, where I attended Palm Beach Atlantic University. I was 18 years old and had discovered a new freedom I never had. It was also here that I had discovered alcohol, my drug of choice. Somehow, I was able to keep up my grades adequately despite the careless lifestyle I began to live.

Later, I decided to join the Marine Corps, where I learned true physical and mental discipline. This enabled me to satisfy the sense of adventure I so desperately hungered for.

Skip ahead a few years. I got a job in the biomedical technology field. My career began to advance. I was dating the most wonderful woman I had ever met, Jennifer. I eventually asked her to marry me. Through some wonder, she said yes. God does do miracles!

I landed a position as a field engineer for a top imaging company. This position was 100% travel, which offered me opportunities to visit places I would never otherwise have been able to visit. My first child, Julia, was born and life could not be better. It's been said that the greatest gift from above is a daughter for her daddy to love.

We attended Community Christian Church in West Palm Beach, where I served on the praise and worship team and eventually became a deacon. Life was great. Then I received a double portion of blessings when my second daughter, Katelyn, was born. I could not have been happier. I was living the dream—beautiful wife, dream job, 2 lovely daughters, nice house, cars and time to spend.

All along, however, for reasons unknown except to turn off my mind, I really enjoyed having a drink after the family went to sleep. At first it was just a few times a week, but the hook was set. One thing led to another and before I knew it, I was being sneaky and drinking every night. I thought I was being stealthy enough to hide the amount and frequency, but my wife knew all along. She pleaded with me to stop. She knew I had a problem many years before I was even willing to admit to it.

She did all the work for me to get professional help. She even had my two brothers come to South Florida to intervene. "No," I thought. "I am bigger than this...I can do this on my own." At the time, surrender was not in my creed.

Several short spans of sobriety followed by increasingly more relapses seemed to be the cycle for the next few years. The addiction was full blown. I went through 2 – 30 day programs, but still the relapses were soon to follow only getting progressively worse. I was circling the drain but still too stubborn to surrender. At one point, I even remember thinking to myself, "I got this," even though I was killing myself.

What makes this disease so shrewd is that it tells you that you are OK when you really are not. God said, "OK, Rick, let's do it your way." The next day, I was pulled over for speeding. I blew a .26 and was charged with a DUI. A few months before this, my wife had filed for divorce. She saw me going down a path of self-destruction that she simply could not be a part of.

I was finished. All was lost.

The next day, I called a friend of mine from a men's group at my church. He had been witnessing my self-destruction and told me that I was in desperate need of a life changing experience. I showed up at Faith Farm with nothing to show but my suitcase. *The Purpose Driven Life* states that, "You'll never know that God is all you need until God is all you've got."

There is good news, because God is sovereign and in control of all events and incidents in His plan for us. Everything that happens to us has spiritual significance. If tragedy is needed in your life in order for you to come closer to God, He will not hesitate to allow that to happen.

Romans 8:28 states,

> *We know that God causes everything to work together for the good of those who love God and are called according to His purpose. (NLT)*

So, I show up at Faith Farm on a Friday morning, just in time to view a video. This Faith Farm thing isn't so bad, I thought. I was told I would be part of the landscape maintenance specialists, a/k/a Lawn Crew! We don't have cattle or orange groves here, but we do seem to grow a great deal of grass. I assumed I would be driving a tractor with an air-conditioned cabin. Never did find that tractor. Pushing a lawn mower and trying to start a 15 year old weed eater during the hottest part of the summer allowed me to sweat out all of my sins.

Then I was told I was going to be transferred to the store to be an associate in our outside sales department. Evidently, God does have a sense of humor. Here I learned patience, tolerance, perseverance and longsuffering. I could sell a $3.00 end table like there was no tomorrow.

Finally, I made it to my current home; electronics. Here I learned that the Bible really means all things are decent and in order. You see, it is very important that you first unplug electronics prior to cutting the electrical cord ... and it must be done in that order! Failure to do so will lead to a very shocking experience.

When I got to Faith Farm I was desperate. I was completely broken. I learned to surrender. Having lost everything, I learned to cast all my cares on Christ, for He cares for me. I learned that my way isn't the best way and is surely not God's way. My very soul was restless and irritable.

If you are out there listening to me right now and can feel a connection to that feeling, I would like to offer you something that worked for me. This is something that was soothing and gave me the comfort and peace that I craved. Pick up your Bible and start reading and meditating on God's Word. I can't give you a solid explanation but you realize that peace that passes understanding, just as Scripture states.

Class 5 will be here before you know it. You will do some deep soul searching and self-development. You will also learn the tactics of the adversary. Know your enemy. This knowledge is extremely important for the future. Now you will be armed and be able to defend yourself spiritually from attacks by the adversary instead of turning to a chemical.

Julius Caesar once said, *"Si vis pacem, parabellum."* If you seek peace, prepare for war. Today I stand before you a new creation.

Theresa

I'd like to start by saying that my life is a true testimony of the grace of God. I grew up in New Jersey and had a normal childhood. As an adult, I made choices that would change the course of my life.

I went through life with no hope at all and accepted the fact that I was a drug addict. I believed I could be nothing more. I was nothing more. I acted out in self-destructive ways, and needless to say, I made a mess of my life. I have been married, divorced, beaten up, shot at, homeless and slept on cardboard boxes.

You see, I was fighting an addiction so powerful that it took over every aspect of my life. I turned my back on my family and my two children. But worst of all, I turned my back on the Lord. I had lost all hope and self-respect. Romans 6:21 states,

> *What benefit did you reap at that time from the things you are now ashamed of? Those things result in death!*
> *(GNT)*

Finally, the Lord showed mercy on me. I was arrested and went to prison. Sadly, my life was so bad that prison was a blessing at that time. Psalm 41-42 states,

> *I waited patiently for the Lord's help. Then He listened to me and heard my cry. He pulled me out of the dangerous pit, out of the deadly quick sand. He set me safely on a rock and made me secure. (GNT)*

I believe that what the devil intended to use to destroy me, God is using for His glory.

What I've been through is what made me the women I am today, and I can do all things in Christ who strengthens me. Philippians 3:13 declares,

> *Forgetting what is behind and straining toward what is ahead.* (GNT)

While in prison, I developed a relationship with the Lord. One day in my cell, I got down on my knees and prayed. I said, "Lord I'm tired of doing things my way. Please let your will be done." After that day, my life started changing drastically. My relationship with my family was restored, and I finally had peace in my life. I actually liked the person I was becoming.

Upon my release from prison, I made the decision to come to Faith Farm. It was the best decision I ever made. My faith in the Lord and coming to Faith Farm has truly saved my life. By the grace of God, I've been free of drugs and alcohol for 2 years and 10 months. Don't get me wrong, I'm still a work in progress, but Christ has set me free. We may doubt our own abilities and potential, but never doubt what God can do when we give our trust and obedience to Him.

In closing, I'd like to thank my family for never giving up on me, for showing me tough love whenever I needed it and for loving me enough to forgive me once again.

To the Pastor, Sister Debbie and Staff, I'd like to quote Hebrews *6:10,*

> *God is fair. He will not forget the work you did and the love you showed for Him by helping His people.*

Thank you and please keep me in your prayers.

Matthew

Author's Note: *In lieu of incarceration in prison, the Judge sentenced Matthew to Faith Farm in a "house arrest" status. That meant he could not sleep in the dorm with the other men because the electronic signal on his house arrest device could not be received by the police through the dorm roof. Therefore, Matthew had to sleep in the dorm breezeway where the signal from the device could be picked up and monitoried by authorities, to verify his presence on the Faith Farm campus.*

Webster's Dictionary defines "integrity" as: *A state of being complete, unbroken and unimpaired with sound moral, principle, honesty, sincerity, uprightness and being sound.*

My years of drug addiction were but a symptom of the real issue; my lack of integrity. This manifested the self-centeredness, selfishness and rebellion against God and anybody else that got in my way. For all the trials I had been through in my life, I think of Job; a man of God and a man of great integrity, who said,

> *Shall we, indeed, accept good from God? Shall we not accept adversity?*

I didn't accept good let alone the adversity.

It's kind of hard to put a 20-year addiction into 5 minutes. But I'll give it a whirl. I was raised in a wealthy Jewish family, the youngest child of an alcoholic father and a bulimic mother. On the outside, things looked good. But, there was definitely some dysfunction going on in there. Even so, I did have a pretty good childhood. I lacked nothing material and I was loved by my parents and sisters; and I loved them. Yet I always felt restless, irritable, discontent, and most of all, inadequate.

Anyway, at the age of 14, my parents divorced. At age 15, my father committed suicide; a crushing blow to an adolescent boy trudging through the awkwardness of becoming a man. Needless to say, I turned to using drugs and relationships to fill the emptiness, the rejection and the inadequacy that ruled my soul.

At that time, I became an atheist … if I even believed in God to begin with. So over the next 15 years or so, I self-medicated with various drugs to kill the pain of life, getting approval from playing in bands. I sought relationships to feel accepted. Eventually, I turned to injecting heroin, which I never thought I would do because it was like something you see on a 1970s B-rated movie or something like that; some episode of *Baretta*!

Anyways, I was ensnared by its evil gain and promise of comfort. It was a lie. I became a full-blown addict, a liar, a cheat, a thief; and I landed a 5-year prison sentence. I did get clean in prison for half of it, and at that time, I researched a lot of religions and started believing. At that time, I became an agnostic. I figured something or someone was out there watching over me. In retrospect, God was calling me to Him, but my heart was way too hardened.

I did well when I was released. I went to school, stayed clean and met a beautiful woman who became my wife. We had 2 boys, bought a home and I stayed employed for the most part. But the lack of integrity, once again, led to yet a worse relapse of oxycodone and then heroin. During that era I became a Christian thanks to my wife who made me go to church. I went from a Jew to an atheist, to an agnostic and to a Christian; and I was like… that's pretty weird. I've experienced it all.

I gave my heart to Christ with my wife, but I was still lacking the main ingredient … integrity. And, I refused to give up everything for Him. Also during that kind of strange period of time in my life, I landed a record contract. I toured the country, was on the radio, in magazines and played in front of thousands of people. I had adoration of people and acceptance. I had arrived. It was great.

Actually, it was infidelity; on the verge of a divorce, loneliness, extreme alcohol and opiate abuse, exalting myself and lack of humility. Not as enchanting as I thought; be careful what you wish for ... you just might get it.

Again, God was calling me. I felt so convicted during that time. I walked away from it. I walked away from the band, the record company and the lifestyle to save my marriage and my life. And it sounds great. It sounds honorable. But what I walked away with was a huge resentment and an identity crisis. I didn't know who I was because playing music was who I thought I was ... not what I did.

Pastor always talks about that. It's not what you do. It's who you are. So, I walked away with resentment and an identity crisis that led to more drugs, lying, cheating, and lo and behold, stealing. I became a thief to support my habit this time. I got caught and accrued a couple more felonies to add to the 15 prior ones I already had. I was finished. The drugs had stopped working. I was dying physically and spiritually.

That was my bottom; not prison and not losing material things. I was an empty shell of a man. I wanted the misery to end and I baker-acted myself. I went cold turkey from a raging heroin habit in a horrible mental ward for 7 days. I did it twice. I baker-acted myself twice! After that, I came to Faith Farm because I had nowhere else to go. At that time, I was facing a minimum of 4 years and a maximum of 10 years in prison, because I had already been to prison and had all these felonies. They were not playing around. I was alone, broken and the walls of my soul were demolished as I sat on that green bench out there. I had nobody. God was the only answer. I tried everything else. Nothing worked. I finally surrendered. Well, I kicked around a little bit, but I was surrendering. I did cry out to God during that period of time and prayed whatever His will, I would do.

At the time, my wife and kids were completely fading away. I was facing prison again and I wanted to run back into the arms of "lack of integrity." Then I thought of Jesus in the Garden as he sweats blood, waiting, knowing what was going to happen to him. He said in Mark 14:36,

> *Abba, Father, all things are possible for You. Take this cup away from me, nevertheless, not what I will, but what You will. (NIV)*

I prayed those words for months, and I meant it … on my knees. No matter what happened, it was God's will. All I wanted was peace. No matter what would happen, I would accept it.

However, as you can see, I'm standing here right now. His will was not for me to go to prison and not for me to lose my family. I had a public defender at the time. After running back and forth from court with my patient and kind mother (very patient … 20 years patient), I only got 10 months house arrest. Hence is why I sleep in the breezeway, so that the police monitors could pick up the electronic signal. I endured 3 months of sleeping on a cot in the breezeway.

I got the 10 months house arrest, which I consider a gift from God. My wife and children, who didn't want anything to do with me, visited me twice a week. My wife and I get along better than we did 9 years ago when we first met. We do have more work to do and trust to build, but we're both focused on God and our own recovery programs. And baby, I wouldn't want to be this happy with anybody else. We used to say something different!

So anyway, Faith Farm is not an easy place to be. I'm not *gonna* be like, "Oh yeah, it's great!" I don't think it was designed to be comfortable. But through God, it saved my life and gave me the opportunity to draw near to God through His precious son, Jesus Christ. The Word of God is God's will for my life. And it's all in the Bible, His will for me. I'm not that double-minded man I used to be. God is real. He loves me, and He's always been with me. I'm grateful to be free from my addiction.

At this time, I would like for my wife and family to stand, all of them that came here to see me graduate. And, I'd like all of my friends here to stand up. Any of the new guys that are here ... why don't you take a look around? I've been here exactly a year, and I had nobody. But these people are my friends, and I love them. And, I love my family, my beautiful wife, thank you. Through You, God has shown me the meaning of grace, because I didn't deserve it. I love you, thank you ... And, the same with you, Mom and Bill. I love you, thank you. And I give all that to the glory of God.

I'm by no means cured. Recovery is a life-long process; my spiritual condition is key, never forgetting where I came from, and most importantly, helping another addict.

In closing, Psalm 40:1-2 says,

> I waited patiently on the Lord and he inclined to me, and heard my cry. He also pulled me out of a horrible pit, out of the miry clay, and set my feet upon a rock.
> (NIV)

That rock is Jesus Christ, the foundation of my life, my recovery and my integrity.

Kristen

Good morning, beautiful church. I am honored to be standing here and to have been chosen by God to be part of the Faith Farm family.

I first want to thank Sister Ann, Sister Epe, Sister Paula and Sisters Gail and Faith with all my heart for all the love, encouragement and time you invested in my life. I also want to thank Pastor and Sister Debbie for coming to the house for communion and Bible studies, and for the Spirit-filled services every week. Also, to my wonderful sisters here, thanks for the many days of laughter and tears, of joy and hardship and for just being there for me. Most of all thanks to my family who have lovingly supported me and made me feel I was still close to home even though I was here. Thanks to those who are helping me get my feet on the ground when I leave today.

Not many of us are living at our best. We linger in the lowlands because we're afraid to climb the mountains. The steepness and ruggedness dismay us. And so we stay in the misty valleys and do not learn the mystery of the hills. We do not know what we lose in our self-indulgence. What glory awaits us, if only we had the courage for the mountain climb. What blessing we should find if only we would move to the uplands of God. And now I would like to share with you a love letter ... a letter from a sinner to her Savior:

My Dear, Dear Lord; You, who created the heavens and the earth and died so that I may live ... Thank you! Oh, thank You Lord for hearing my cry and lifting me out of the miry clay once again. Thank You Lord for setting my feet back on a rock and establishing a firm place for me to stand. I remember clearly kneeling by my bed and

239

crying out loud to You in desperation. I petitioned to You out loud with purpose and conviction to help me.

I was alone and broken. I was losing my home, my health, my self-respect and my dreams. I was on a path going nowhere. Despair and emptiness were my friends. Even though I knew I was one of Yours, my life didn't show the love and peace as only abiding *in* You can give.

I told You I would accept anything You wanted for me, and that no matter what, I would listen and follow the call of Your Spirit. When I prayed that prayer, little did I know You were going to answer my plea ... and not an answer I wanted. Thus began your plan to move me from the island of Key West and place me at Your Faith Farm here in Boynton Beach. I know now that You wanted me to spend quality time with You; sober. I didn't realize how much You loved me, and You were jealous of my time.

I see now that You were not first in my life. Again, I put the pleasures of this world ahead of making You happy and giving You kingship over my life. Drinking became more important than serving You, Lord. I am so sorry that all these times I put my idol first. I didn't realize how sad I made You. Your Holy Spirit grieved as I was blindly going along a path of destruction and falling into the many lies of the enemy. All along You have had Your arms open wide for me to run into.

Instead, I wandered away like the sheep you spoke about in Your Word. I was wandering too far from the flock and had to have my Shepherd come and rescue me. I was near a very steep cliff, too, when You came and pulled me in with your staff and brought me safely back to the flock, and only because I was willing to be obedient and follow what Your will was for my life.

I want to bear much fruit for Your kingdom, Lord. I want to be used as a vessel for Your Spirit. Sin will take you farther than you want to go; Keep you longer than you want to stay; and cost you more than you want to pay! In Proverbs 37:4, Your Word tells me,

Lord, if I delight in You, You will give me the desires of my heart.

And the desires of my heart are to bless you with my life. And in Jeremiah 29:11, it says,

I know the plans I have for you; plans to prosper you and not to harm you; plans to give you hope and a future.

I am excited about my future, Lord, and spending every day of it abiding *IN YOU*. I just want to praise You, my awesome, Holy Lord ... cause You are...

Loving	Sufficient	Just	Merciful
Timeless	Measureless	Invincible	Joyful
Present	Wise	Beautiful	Infinite
Unique	Majestic	Changeless	Wonderful
Spotless	Creative	Forgiving	Accessible
Glorious	Available	Faithful	Sovereign
Holy	Mighty	Powerful	Truthful
Excellent	Steadfast	Peaceful	All-Knowing
Strong	Generous	Radiant	Patient
Reliable	Able	Righteous	Complete
Gracious	Victorious		

Epilogue

Every year on a Sunday in February or March, Faith Farm holds its annual "Homecoming Celebration" at the ninety-acre, Boynton Beach campus. We pitch two huge tents, corner to corner and build a large stage suitable for a nine-piece worship band in the corner where the tents meet. We welcome between 800 to 1,000 graduates of Faith Farm as they return from all over the United States and South America to celebrate their sobriety and what God has done in their lives. We charter commercial busses to bring staff and students from our other campuses. The Faith Tabernacle of Boynton Beach Worship Team leads worship, selected graduates from the three Farms and the Women's Program give updated testimonies on their lives since graduation, and a Keynote Speaker gives a challenge of encouragement. At noon, a prepared BBQ lunch is provided. The afternoon is filled with live music, the annual baseball tournament, tug-of-war games, bounce houses for the kids, kite flying, fishing in the lake, an open mike segment on stage, home-made desserts and great fellowship. A slideshow of historical photos creates nostalgia of past Faith Farm happenings. Alumni are encouraged by the Alumni Association to update their contact information for future contact for fellowship and future gatherings.

We celebrate that they are no longer "takers" from society (stealing for drugs, burglarizing, etc.) but are now "givers" into society through becoming productive citizens. They have a new life in Christ. They have a new life in society.

For years, Faith Farm was a local non-profit organization with mostly south Florida residents as our students. New technology enables people from everywhere to use the Internet to find us for their recovery needs. Since 2008, people from 41 of the 50 states, as well as South America, have entered our program. Although we are physically located in South Florida, we attract from all over the United States and South America. Those who come to this free "Ministry with a Heart for the Hurting" receive non-judgmental acceptance, comfort, unconditional love, work skills and life skills, an accredited recovery program with an opportunity to acquire free college credits, spiritual renewal ... and hope.

FAITH FARM MINISTRIES
"Restoring Hope…. One Life at a Time."
www.faithfarm.org

What Is Faith Farm?

Faith Farm is a free, long term, residential drug and alcohol recovery program whose motto is:

"A Ministry with a Heart for the Hurting."

Since its establishment in 1951 by Rev. Garland "Pappy" Eastham, Faith Farm has been helping men and women who want a transformation in their lives from drug and alcohol addiction to a new, sober lifestyle with spiritual renewal.

Faith Farm has a total of over 1,600 acres located at three south Florida campuses: Our "Urban Model" with 13 acres in Ft. Lauderdale (Broward County); the "Suburban Model" with 90 acres in Boynton Beach (Palm Beach County); and the "Rural Model" with 1,500 acres in Okeechobee (Okeechobee County). Finally, housed at the Boynton Beach location, is our "Women's Model", known as Eastham Home for Women. In all, there are 445 beds, with 417 beds for men and 28 beds for women.

The basic, minimum 9-month program is a work training program. Students have a structured regimen each day from lights on to lights out time; morning chapel, classroom instruction and an assigned work project. In the classroom, they learn about addiction, setting boundaries, anger management, spiritual training and other core subjects.

Faith Farm's free recovery program is accredited through our partnership with South Florida Bible College and Theological Seminary, which enables our students to earn up to 9-college credit hours for their Faith Farm classroom time by passing an exam at the end of their recovery program.

Students' work projects consist of one or more of the following: Thrift store sales; New Furniture sales; Trucks & Dock; Dairy Calves; Cattle & Grove Operations; Food Service; Call Center Operations; Landscape Maintenance; Auto Repair; Security; Basic Computer; Salvage; Appliance Repair; Facility Maintenance; Janitorial Services; and Instructor. These categories make up our Comprehensive Work Training (CWT) Program, which provides Resumé-worthy skills and Certificates of Training as evidence of mastered skills in 15 different job areas. These skills feature both classroom instruction, and on-the-job training. Combined with resume, application and interview skills training, they are well prepared for the competitive job market upon graduation.

A GED education is mandatory if a high school diploma has not yet been achieved. The goal is to get them back on their feet, physically, mentally, and spiritually. The long-term program that keeps students off the streets and cocooned in love allows regeneration of spirit and desire while setting a new life course.

Although all three Farms are located in South Florida, Faith Farm has a national outreach. Since 2008, we have admitted students from 82% (41 of 50) of the states, plus South America. We have had every occupation: The CIA in Washington; top hotel chefs from Miami Beach; ex-millionaires; and homeless and convicted felons as students at Faith Farm.

Educationally, we have had students with a 4th grade education who could not read to students with Doctorate Degrees. One of our students spoke seven languages fluently. Economically, we have had homeless students with nothing to those who had been multi-millionaires, but lost everything due to their addiction. We have had those who were injured in an auto accident, prescribed pain medications, and then became addicted. As a result they lost their jobs, family and assets.

Spiritually, we have had students off the streets, who have never been to church or read a Bible; all they knew about God was in swear-words. At the other end of the spectrum are those who were raised in a good Christian or Jewish home, but got side-tracked by peer pressure. "Experimenting" with drugs or alcohol led to an addiction. They are reminded that our thoughts determine feelings, and our feelings then control our actions. We have had students come from fundamental Christian homes, Catholic and Jewish upbringing and Muslim backgrounds, as well as those with no faith at all.

We speak to each incoming class and tell them that it is never too late to begin to leave a positive legacy. They are reminded that they are remembered not by how they *start*, but how they *finish* in life. We urge them to take advantage of all that Faith Farm offers and to finish well. We hope that reading these testimonies of those that made a "U-TURN" in life are an encouragement to you and will provide comfort that there is always hope. We are working daily to transform lives out of the darkness and into the light.

Dean O. Webb, Executive Director
Faith Farm Ministries

Campus Locations

Map of Florida

Our National Outreach

A ministry with a heart for the hurting

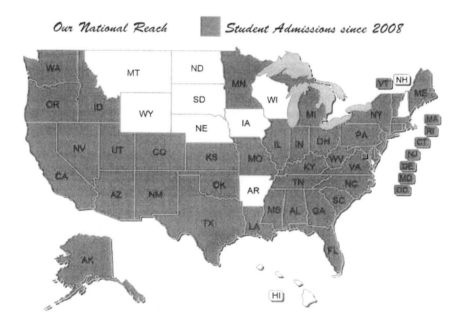

Our National Reach *Student Admissions since 2008*

Although all three campuses are in South Florida, in the last five years we have had students come from forty-one of fifty U.S. states and from South America.

About Our Founder

This book is about the changed lives that occurred because of a man of faith, Rev. Garland Eastham, affectionately known as *"Pappy"*, who founded Faith Farm Ministries. In 1951, "Pappy" came to Ft. Lauderdale, Florida, and began a church called Fort Lauderdale Rescue Tabernacle, Inc., known as a *"House of Prayer"*. He took people off the street overnight; gave them food, a shower, a gospel message and a clean bed to sleep in.

Rev. Garland "Pappy" Eastham
Founder of Faith Farm Ministries

Night after night, he saw the same people coming back without any change in their lifestyle. So, he decided to lengthen the stay in order to have more positive input into their lives and effect a more permanent change. To do that, he created a longer term program at the current 13-acre parcel in Ft. Lauderdale. They began to grow vegetables and landscaping plant material. They also began to fix up furniture and sell it to provide the funds needed to house the men in the program. It became known as "Faith Farm Ministries."

Over time, the program was gradually lengthened to 9 months. There was now enough time to give meaningful input into men's lives through a structured environment, teachings and experiences of Christ's love and forgiveness.

The waiting list grew longer and Rev. Eastham expanded further with the purchase of 90 acres located in Boynton Beach in Palm Beach County. As street drug use became joined to alcohol use, the need for recovery grew more severe. Both the Ft. Lauderdale and Boynton Beach campuses became outgrown, and an additional 1,500 acres were purchased in Okeechobee County. In recent years, we've added the problem of addictions to pain killers and other prescription medications as further need for Faith Farm's Regeneration Program.

Today, the three campuses have a capacity of 445 beds, and minister to 417 men and 28 women. As the realm of addictions within our society continues to grow; from alcohol and illegal drugs to pain medications and other prescription drugs, the need for the programs at Faith Farm continues to increase as well. Yet, throughout these 63 years, "Pappy's" vision remains viable to this day. Rev. Eastham's concept of a substance abuse recovery program that encourages individual responsibility and accountability is based in faith, provides education and work training and continues to be a model for changed lives.

Dean O. Webb, Executive Director
Faith Farm Ministries
www.FaithFarm.org

To learn more about Faith Farm Ministries' recovery program, micro-enterprise, college accreditation or Comprehensive Work Training (CWT Institute), please visit our website:

www.FaithFarm.org

Partner with us.
Click on the "Ways To Give" Tab.